Depression

DEPRESSION

Your Questions Answered

Romeo Vitelli

Q&A Health Guides

An Imprint of ABC-CLIO, LLC
Santa Barbara, California • Denver, Colorado

Copyright © 2019 by ABC-CLIO, LLC

Library of Congress Cataloging in Publication Control Number: 2019941511

ISBN: 978-1-4408-6600-5 (print)

    978-1-4408-6601-2 (ebook)

23 22 21 20 19   1 2 3 4 5

This book is also available as an eBook.

Greenwood
An Imprint of ABC-CLIO, LLC

ABC-CLIO, LLC
147 Castilian Drive
Santa Barbara, California 93117
www.abc-clio.com

This book is printed on acid-free paper ∞

Manufactured in the United States of America

This book is dedicated to Dr. Norman S. Endler whose own holiday of darkness helped inspire this book. It is also dedicated to all of my clients dealing with depression, and I thank you for the insights you have provided. May this book help others find a way to come to terms with their depression and get on with their lives.

Contents

Series Foreword

All of us have questions about our health. Is this normal? Should I be doing something differently? Whom should I talk to about my concerns? And our modern world is full of answers. Thanks to the Internet, there's a wealth of information at our fingertips, from forums where people can share their personal experiences to Wikipedia articles to the full text of medical studies. But finding the right information can be an intimidating and difficult task—some sources are written at too high a level, others have been oversimplified, while still others are heavily biased or simply inaccurate.

Q&A Health Guides address the needs of readers who want accurate, concise answers to their health questions, authored by reputable and objective experts, and written in clear and easy-to-understand language. This series focuses on the topics that matter most to young adult readers, including various aspects of physical and emotional well-being as well as other components of a healthy lifestyle. These guides will also serve as a valuable tool for parents, school counselors, and others who may need to answer teens' health questions.

All books in the series follow the same format to make finding information quick and easy. Each volume begins with an essay on health literacy and why it is so important when it comes to gathering and evaluating health information. Next, the top five myths and misconceptions that surround the topic are dispelled. The heart of each guide is a collection of questions and answers, organized thematically. A selection of five case studies provides real-world examples to illuminate key concepts. Rounding out each volume are a directory of resources, a glossary, and an index.

It is our hope that the books in this series will not only provide valuable information but will also help guide readers toward a lifetime of healthy decision-making.

Acknowledgments

I would like to thank the various researchers and therapists whose efforts have helped make this book possible. Thanks also go to Maxine Taylor of ABC-CLIO and their excellent support staff as well as those colleagues of mine who were kind enough to review sections of this book and provide helpful suggestions on how it could be improved.

Introduction

Depression is like a heaviness that you can't ever escape. It crushes down on you, making even the smallest things like tying your shoes or chewing on toast seem like a twenty-mile hike uphill. Depression is a part of you; it's in your bones and your blood.

Jasmine Warga

If there is any mental health issue that can be said to be universal, it's depression. Among the famous people who dealt with this crippling disease were such luminaries as Edgar Allen Poe, Winston Churchill, Abraham Lincoln, and Virginia Woolf, to name just a few. But depression has been found in people of all ages and cultures and in just about every era in human history. For that matter, it may *predate* human history considering that depressive symptoms have been observed in numerous nonhuman species as well.

We all get depressed, at least once in a while, though for most people, those "blue moods" pass quickly enough. But not everyone is so lucky. In the United States alone, mood disorders are the most common reason for children from one to seventeen years of age to be hospitalized, and more than fifty thousand Medicaid patients are readmitted to hospital for depression each year. And these grim statistics are in line with what is being reported in most other industrialized countries as well.

Unfortunately, getting accurate statistics is often impossible in many countries because the stigma attached to most forms of mental illness, including depression, often encourages people to suffer in silence. In most developing nations, psychiatrists are in extremely short supply, and psychiatric help is simply not available for many patients courageous enough to ask for it. Even in supposedly advanced nations like the United States, the long waiting lists for proper treatment can lead to depressed people having to wait months to get help, even if it's just in the form of medication.

Much of the stigma surrounding depression stems from a basic misunderstanding of what depression actually *is*. Even for people with mild depression, the failure to "just get over it" often leads to feelings of guilt or shame due to not being able to handle the symptoms on their own. And for the ones dealing with more severe symptoms, getting help means months, or even years, of experimentation to find the right treatment. For that matter, horrifying stories of depression being treated through exorcisms or spurious local remedies, which often do more harm than good, are disturbingly common, even in countries where better options exist.

Along with psychotherapy, use of various herbal remedies to treat depression has a very long history, but now that we are in the "Age of Prozac," is it any surprise that antidepressants are the most commonly prescribed medication of all? With an estimated sixteen million people on antidepressants in the United States alone, the sheer demand for better and stronger antidepressants has provided a permanent and growing source of revenue for pharmaceutical companies. And the demand for newer and better drugs has soared over the past few decades.

Still, despite the various treatment options now available, depression continues to be a major health issue worldwide. Whether it leads to suicide, substance abuse, destroyed marriages, or lost jobs, the physical and economic toll of depression cannot be underestimated. Unfortunately, while depression is something that everyone has experience with, there are far too many misconceptions on what it is and how it should be treated. For example, many people confuse depression with the feelings of sadness that we all experience from time to time, and they often think that overcoming depression is just a matter of "snapping out of it" through sheer willpower. Nothing could be further from the truth.

In my new book, *Depression: Your Questions Answered*, I address many misconceptions about depression and discuss how damaging these widely held beliefs can be. I discuss the different controversies surrounding depression as well as how depression can be effectively diagnosed and treated.

This book is also intended to provide basic answers to many of the most common questions people are likely to ask about depression and is broken down into different sections to help readers focus on what is most important to them. The material covered in this book should help those dealing with depression themselves, their family members, concerned friends, and even health professionals seeking further information to help patients dealing with this crippling disorder.

For far too many people dealing with depression and their families, there is often a sense of pessimism that depression is something that cannot be overcome for long. This is far from the case, however, as countless success stories have shown, some of which will be mentioned in this book. The most critical thing people dealing with depression need to remember is to never give up hope. The right help is out there; you just need to be willing to find it.

Guide to Health Literacy

On her 13th birthday, Samantha was diagnosed with type 2 diabetes. She consulted her mom and her aunt, both of whom also have type 2 diabetes, and decided to go with their strategy of managing diabetes by taking insulin. As a result of participating in an after-school program at her middle school that focused on health literacy, she learned that she can help manage the level of glucose in her bloodstream by counting her carbohydrate intake, following a diabetic diet, and exercising regularly. But, what exactly should she do? How does she keep track of her carbohydrate intake? What is a diabetic diet? How long should she exercise, and what type of exercise should she do? Samantha is a visual learner, so she turned to her favorite source of media, YouTube, to answer these questions. She found videos from individuals around the world sharing their experiences and tips, doctors (or at least people who have "Dr." in their YouTube channel names), government agencies such as the National Institutes of Health, and even video clips from cat lovers who have cats with diabetes. With guidance from the librarian and the health and science teachers at her school, she assessed the credibility of the information in these videos and even compared their suggestions to some of the print resources that she was able to find at her school library. Now, she knows exactly how to count her carbohydrate level, how to prepare and follow a diabetic diet, and how much (and what) exercise is needed daily. She intends to share her findings with her mom and her aunt, and now she wants to create a chart that summarizes what she has learned that she can share with her doctor.

Samantha's experience is not unique. She represents a shift in our society; an individual no longer views himself or herself as a passive recipient of medical care but as an active mediator of his or her own health. However, in this era when any individual can post his or her opinions and experiences with a particular health condition online with just a few clicks or publish a memoir, it is vital that people know how to assess the credibility of health information. Gone are the days when "publishing" health information required intense vetting. The health information landscape is highly saturated, and people have innumerable sources where they can find information about practically any health topic. The sources (whether print, online, or a person) that an individual consults for health information are crucial because the accuracy and trustworthiness of the information can potentially affect his or her overall health. The ability to find, select, assess, and use health information constitutes a type of literacy—health literacy—that everyone must possess.

THE DEFINITION AND PHASES OF HEALTH LITERACY

One of the most popular definitions for health literacy comes from Ratzan and Parker (2000), who describe health literacy as "the degree to which individuals have the capacity to obtain, process, and understand basic health information and services needed to make appropriate health decisions." Recent research has extrapolated health literacy into health literacy bits, further shedding light on the multiple phases and literacy practices that are embedded within the multifaceted concept of health literacy. Although this research has focused primarily on online health information seeking, these health literacy bits are needed to successfully navigate both print and online sources. There are six phases of health information seeking: (1) Information Need Identification and Question Formulation, (2) Information Search, (3) Information Comprehension, (4) Information Assessment, (5) Information Management, and (6) Information Use.

The first phase is the *information need identification and question formulation phase*. In this phase, one needs to be able to develop and refine a range of questions to frame one's search and understand relevant health terms. In the second phase, *information search*, one has to possess appropriate searching skills, such as using proper keywords and correct spelling in search terms, especially when using search engines and databases. It is also crucial to understand how search engines work (i.e., how search results are derived, what the order of the search results means, how to use the snippets that are provided in the search results list to select websites, and how to determine which listings are ads on a search engine results page). One also has to limit reliance on surface characteristics, such as the design of a website or a book (a website or book that appears to have a lot of information or looks aesthetically pleasant does not necessarily mean it has good information) and language used (a website or book that utilizes jargon, the keywords that one used to conduct the search, or the word "information" does not necessarily indicate it will have good information). The next phase is *information comprehension*, whereby one needs to have the ability to read, comprehend, and recall the information (including textual, numerical, and visual content) one has located from the books and/or online resources.

To assess the credibility of health information (*information assessment* phase), one needs to be able to evaluate information for accuracy, evaluate how current the information is (e.g., when a website was last updated or when a book was published), and evaluate the creators of the source—for example, examine site sponsors or type of sites (.com,. gov,. edu, or. org) or the author of a book (practicing doctor, a celebrity doctor, a patient of a specific disease, etc.) to determine the believability of the person/ organization providing the information. Such credibility perceptions tend to become generalized, so they must be frequently reexamined (e.g., the belief that a specific news agency always has credible health information needs continuous vetting). One also needs to evaluate the credibility of the medium (e.g., television, Internet, radio, social media, and book) and evaluate—not just accept without questioning—others' claims regarding the validity of a site, book, or other specific source of information. At this stage, one has to "make sense of information gathered from diverse sources by identifying misconceptions, main and supporting ideas, conflicting information, point of view, and biases" (American Association of School Librarians [AASL], 2009, p. 13) and conclude which sources/ information are valid and accurate by using conscious strategies rather than simply using intuitive judgments or "rules of thumb." This phase is the most challenging segment of health information seeking and serves as a determinant of success (or lack thereof) in the information-seeking process. The following section on Sources of Health Information further explains this phase.

The fifth phase is *information management*, whereby one has to organize information that has been gathered in some manner to ensure easy retrieval and use in the future. The last phase is *information use*, in which one will synthesize information found across various resources, draw conclusions, and locate the answer to his or her original question and/or the content that fulfills the information need. This phase also often involves implementation, such as using the information to solve a health problem; make health-related decisions; identify and engage in behaviors that will help a person to avoid health risks; share the health information found with family members and friends who may benefit from it; and advocate more broadly for personal, family, or community health.

THE IMPORTANCE OF HEALTH LITERACY

The conception of health has moved from a passive view (someone is either well or ill) to one that is more active and process based (someone is working toward preventing or managing disease). Hence, the dominant focus has shifted from doctors and treatments to patients and prevention, resulting in the need to strengthen our ability and confidence (as patients and consumers of health care) to look for, assess, understand, manage, share, adapt, and use health-related information. An individual's health literacy level has been found to predict his or her health status better than age, race, educational attainment, employment status, and income level (National Network of Libraries of Medicine, 2013). Greater health literacy also enables individuals to better communicate with health care providers such as doctors, nutritionists, and therapists, as they can pose more relevant, informed, and useful questions to health care providers. Another added advantage of greater health literacy is better information-seeking skills, not only for health but also in other domains, such as completing assignments for school.

SOURCES OF HEALTH INFORMATION: THE GOOD, THE BAD, AND THE IN-BETWEEN

For generations, doctors, nurses, nutritionists, health coaches, and other health professionals have been the trusted sources of health information. Additionally, researchers have found that young adults, when they have health-related questions, typically turn to a family member who has had firsthand experience with a health condition because of their family member's close proximity and because of their past experience with, and trust in, this individual. Expertise should be a core consideration when consulting a person, website, or book for health information. The credentials and background of the person or author and conflicting interests of the author (and his or her organization) must be checked and validated to ensure the likely credibility of the health information they are conveying. While books often have implied credibility because of the peer-review process involved, self-publishing has challenged this credibility, so qualifications of book authors should also be verified. When it comes to health information, currency of the source must also be examined. When examining health information/studies presented, pay attention to the exhaustiveness of research methods utilized to offer recommendations or conclusions. Small and nondiverse sample size is often—but not always—an indication of reduced credibility. Studies that confuse correlation with causation is another potential issue to watch for. Information seekers must also pay attention to the sponsors of the research studies. For example, if a study is sponsored by manufacturers of drug Y and the study recommends that drug Y is the best treatment to manage or cure a disease, this may indicate a lack of objectivity on the part of the researchers.

The Internet is rapidly becoming one of the main sources of health information. Online forums, news agencies, personal blogs, social media sites, pharmacy sites, and celebrity "doctors" are all offering medical and health information targeted to various types of people in regard to all types of diseases and symptoms. There are professional journalists, citizen journalists, hoaxers, and people paid to write fake health news on various sites that may appear to have a legitimate domain name and may even have authors who claim to have professional credentials, such as an MD. All these sites *may* offer useful information or information that appears to be useful and relevant; however, much of the information may be debatable and may fall into gray areas that require readers to discern credibility, reliability, and biases.

While broad recognition and acceptance of certain media, institutions, and people often serve as the most popular determining factors to assess credibility of health information among young people, keep in mind that there are legitimate Internet sites, databases, and books that publish health information and serve as sources of health information for doctors, other health sites, and members of the public. For example, MedlinePlus (https://medlineplus.gov) has trusted sources on over 975 diseases and conditions and presents the information in easy-to-understand language.

The chart here presents factors to consider when assessing credibility of health information. However, keep in mind that these factors function only as a guide and require continuous updating to keep abreast with the changes in the landscape of health information, information sources, and technologies.

The chart can serve as a guide; however, approaching a librarian about how one can go about assessing the credibility of both print and online

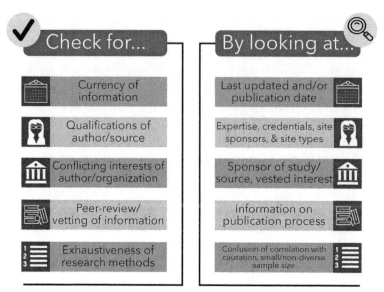

All images from flaticon.com

health information is far more effective than using generic checklist-type tools. While librarians are not health experts, they can apply and teach patrons strategies to determine the credibility of health information.

With the prevalence of fake sites and fake resources that appear to be legitimate, it is important to use the following health information assessment tips to verify health information that one has obtained (St. Jean et al., 2015, p. 151):

- **Don't assume you are right**: Even when you feel very sure about an answer, keep in mind that the answer may not be correct, and it is important to conduct (further) searches to validate the information.
- **Don't assume you are wrong**: You may actually have correct information, even if the information you encounter does not match—that is, you may be right and the resources that you have found may contain false information.
- **Take an open approach**: Maintain a critical stance by not including your preexisting beliefs as keywords (or letting them influence your choice of keywords) in a search, as this may influence what it is possible to find out.
- **Verify, verify, and verify**: Information found, especially on the Internet, needs to be validated, no matter how the information appears on

the site (i.e., regardless of the appearance of the site or the quantity of information that is included).

Health literacy comes with experience navigating health information. Professional sources of health information, such as doctors, health care providers, and health databases, are still the best, but one also has the power to search for health information and then verify it by consulting with these trusted sources and by using the health information assessment tips and guide shared previously.

Mega Subramaniam, PhD
Associate Professor, College of Information
Studies, University of Maryland

REFERENCES AND FURTHER READING

American Association of School Librarians (AASL). (2009). *Standards for the 21st-century learner in action*. Chicago, IL: American Association of School Librarians.

Hilligoss, B., & Rieh, S.-Y. (2008). Developing a unifying framework of credibility assessment: Construct, heuristics, and interaction in context. *Information Processing & Management, 44*(4), 1467–1484.

Kuhlthau, C. C. (1988). Developing a model of the library search process: Cognitive and affective aspects. *Reference Quarterly, 28*(2), 232–242.

National Network of Libraries of Medicine (NNLM). (2013). Health literacy. Bethesda, MD: National Network of Libraries of Medicine. Retrieved from nnlm.gov/outreach/consumer/hlthlit.html

Ratzan, S. C., & Parker, R. M. (2000). Introduction. In C. R. Selden, M. Zorn, S. C. Ratzan, & R. M. Parker (Eds.), *National Library of Medicine current bibliographies in medicine: Health literacy*. NLM Pub. No. CBM 2000-1. Bethesda, MD: National Institutes of Health, U.S. Department of Health and Human Services.

St. Jean, B., Subramaniam, M., Taylor, N. G., Follman, R., Kodama, C., & Casciotti, D. (2015). The influence of positive hypothesis testing on youths' online health-related information seeking. *New Library World, 116*(3/4), 136–154.

St. Jean, B., Taylor, N. G., Kodama, C., & Subramaniam, M. (February 2017). Assessing the health information source perceptions of tweens using card-sorting exercises. *Journal of Information Science, 44*(2): 148–164. Retrieved from http://journals.sagepub.com/doi/abs/10.1177/0165551516687728

Subramaniam, M., St. Jean, B., Taylor, N.G., Kodama, C., Follman, R., & Casciotti, D. (2015). Bit by bit: Using design-based research to improve the health literacy of adolescents. *JMIR Research Protocols, 4*(2), paper e62. Retrieved from http://www.ncbi.nlm.nih.gov/pmc/articles/PMC4464334/

Valenza, J. (2016, November 26). Truth, truthiness, and triangulation: A news literacy toolkit for a "post-truth" world [Web log]. Retrieved from http://blogs.slj.com/neverendingsearch/2016/11/26/truth-truthiness-triangulation-and-the-librarian-way-a-news-literacy-toolkit-for-a-post-truth-world/

Common Misconceptions about Depression

1. DEPRESSION IS ALL IN YOUR HEAD

One of the reasons so many people have trouble taking depression seriously is that it is a largely invisible disorder. Despite being able to describe the symptoms you might be feeling, there are no independent medical tests that can be used to prove that you are really depressed. As a result, depressed people are often told they can simply "get over it" if they try hard enough and, if that doesn't work, that they are somehow at fault for not being sufficiently strong-willed or are just seeking attention. Even family doctors may just prescribe a medication such as Prozac in the hope of solving the problem without exploring the underlying reasons for the depression. Question 2 offers an overview of the different types of clinically diagnosable depression.

2. DEPRESSION IS THE SAME AS SADNESS

While everyone may think they know what depression is, they are usually just talking about specific symptoms such as sadness or chronic fatigue. Even though these symptoms are often found in clinical depression, it's important not to assume that having these symptoms mean that you are suffering from depression. And, just as importantly, it is quite possible to be suffering from clinical depression even if you *aren't* feeling these specific symptoms. As one example, feeling sad is a normal part of the human existence and can occur whenever we experience a setback or some sort of disappointment. For people dealing with depression, problems with emotional numbing or despondency may prevent any kind of natural emotions from coming out, including feelings of sadness or joy. Considering how complicated the process of diagnosing depression can be, this needs to be left up to a trained mental health professional. Question 3 provides more information about the differences between sadness and depression.

3. ONLY WEAK PEOPLE GET DEPRESSED

This is one of the most heartbreaking misconceptions faced by people dealing with depression. Many otherwise well-meaning people have difficulty accepting that depression is a disease and feel that people dealing with depression simply lack the willpower to get over it. Whether due to genetics, upbringing, poor environment, or emotional problems stemming from trauma, many people are particularly vulnerable to depression and accusing them of lacking self-control makes recovery much harder than it needs to be. As we will see in later sections of this book, depression isn't just a matter of "getting the blues," and it isn't something that only happens to people who aren't strong enough to "get over it" (as far too many friends and family members might wrongly suggest). Rather than being a sign of weakness, dealing with depression often means forcing yourself to get out of bed, dress yourself, and still do all the things you need to do, even while you wonder why you should make the effort. Coming to terms with these feelings and forcing yourself to keep going, not to mention finding the energy to find help when you need it, is the very opposite of weakness. Only someone who experiences clinical depression can truly understand this. Question 5 discusses which groups of people may be at higher risk of developing clinical depression.

4. CHEERING SOMEONE UP IS THE BEST WAY TO HELP WITH DEPRESSION

Many people, when faced with someone dealing with depression, often have no idea of what to do or say that can make this kind of pain go away. While trying to cheer a depressed person up may seem like the right thing to do, it really isn't. As we've already seen, someone who is clinically depressed isn't just "feeling the blues," and trying to rely on humor or good cheer to make it go away can do more harm than good. If you know someone who is depressed, the best way to help is to *listen* to that person and show that you care about what he or she is going through. Unfortunately, many people may not understand what is happening and, as a result, often find themselves saying the wrong thing or giving bad advice. This is why people who really want to help someone overcome depression needs to start by educating themselves about what depression is and how to help. Reading this book is one way to start, and the Directory of Resources contains other resources as well. For more information about how to get help for yourself or a loved one, see Questions 35, 46, and 47.

5. PEOPLE WHO ARE DEPRESSED ARE "CRAZY"

While clinical depression is considered to be a form of mental illness, that doesn't mean that any of the popular stereotypes about crazy people are going to be true. Most people who are depressed can manage their lives just fine with the right help, whether in the form of medication or counseling (or both, preferably). Depression isn't the same thing as psychosis, and it doesn't necessarily mean that they're inclined to harm themselves or anyone else. Even though some people with depression may begin displaying psychotic symptoms or threaten suicide, this is something that needs to be assessed by a qualified mental health professional who can provide the needed treatment. No matter how worried you are about someone who you know is depressed, you need to respect their own judgment about what is best for them. See Questions 13 to 25 for more information about the many causes and risk factors associated with depression.

QUESTIONS AND ANSWERS

General Information

1. What is depression?

According to the latest version of the *Diagnostic and Statistical Manual of Mental Disorders* (DSM-V), there are a wide range of possible diagnoses that can be given to someone who is clinically depressed. The most common feature of all these conditions is the "presence of sad, empty, or irritable mood, accompanied by somatic or cognitive changes that significantly affect the individual's capacity to function." In other words, it isn't enough just to *feel* depressed; the symptoms also need to be severe enough to prevent sufferers from being able to function, whether on their own, with their families, or at work or school.

But people feeling depressed can experience other symptoms as well. Common symptoms include sadness, irritability, anxiety, apathy, loss of energy, loss of pleasure in things previously enjoyed, changes in sleep and appetite, recurring thoughts of death, physical agitation, feelings of worthlessness, and concentration problems. While all these symptoms can occur in depression, a depressed mood and loss of pleasure are usually considered to be the most common symptoms, and they are the ones most likely to lead to a depression diagnosis.

Though people in their late twenties to mid-thirties seem particularly vulnerable to depression, symptoms can develop at any age. Older adults and even teenagers and young children have been known to commit suicide because they couldn't handle the symptoms they were experiencing.

As we will see in the next question, there are numerous different diagnoses that can be given to someone who is experiencing symptoms of depression. It is typically the job of a qualified mental health professional to make that diagnosis, and over time, the diagnosis can change as well. Though these diagnostic labels can seem arbitrary, they do play a role in the kind of treatment that someone might need to get better and can also provide some clues as to the underlying cause as well.

Among the things a health professional will look at in making an assessment is whether or not the depression has an obvious cause. Many people will develop reactive depression following a traumatic experience or due to grief after the death of a loved one. While this kind of grief is certainly common, it can also lead to a deep depression that may require medication or supportive counseling. On the other hand, depression can also strike out of the blue with no apparent cause at all. This is often called endogenous depression (literally coming from within), though many people developing depression may show signs of both.

But while symptoms of depression can manifest on their own, people suffering from other illnesses, including Parkinson's disease, stroke, multiple sclerosis, and chronic pain, can also become depressed, often to the point of making these conditions far worse than they need to be. Also, older adults who are depressed often develop symptoms that are similar to Alzheimer's disease, at least in the very early stages. This can make early diagnosis very difficult in many cases and may also lead to older patients being afraid to see their doctors about their symptoms.

As we can see, depression can take a variety of different forms depending on how the symptoms reveal themselves. Whatever form these symptoms take, it is essential to see a professional as soon as possible to ensure that the right diagnosis is made and the appropriate treatment is begun.

2. Are there different types of depression?

Some of the confusion that comes from talking about depression is that there are a number of different diagnoses that can be applied depending on the kind of symptoms someone is experiencing, how severe those symptoms are, and the pattern those symptoms follow.

Though these conditions may seem similar in many ways, it is important to leave it up to a qualified mental health professional to make the diagnosis rather than trying to diagnose ourselves or someone we know based on what we might have looked up online. An incorrect diagnosis can mean significant delays in getting the right kind of treatment and lead to unnecessary suffering.

Among the different diagnoses that can be made for someone report-ing symptoms of depression is whether the symptoms are related to true depression or due to bipolar disorder. While we all experience mood swings as we go from highs to lows, these changes in mood tend not to be that severe. With people experiencing bipolar disorder, however, their symptoms often swing from feeling extremely depressed to feeling manic (i.e., superenergized or on top of the world).

Though most manic highs tend not to be that severe (and they are often referred to as hypomanic episodes), people in manic states can often make grandiose plans for the future, talk a mile a minute, and experience an inability to sleep because they are so excited about what is happening to them. They may also be prone to impaired judgment resulting in risky behavior or unwise financial decisions. These manic highs rarely last long though, and as soon as they run their course, the depressive phase sets in.

Since people rarely go to their doctors when they are having a manic episode (and why would they when they feel great?), they are usually only diagnosed after getting in trouble with the law or when family mem-bers force them to get help. The depressive phase, however, can often be impossible to distinguish from true depression. As a result, proper treat-ment can often be delayed, which is why a correct diagnosis is so import-ant, especially in the early stages.

Even when depression is properly diagnosed, there are still different diagnoses that can be given depending on how long the depression lasts and how severe the symptoms are. For people with depression, the most common symptom is major depressive disorder. To receive this diagnosis, someone needs to be experiencing episodes of depression that last for two weeks or more, and depending on how disruptive it is to normal life, it can be classified as severe, moderate, or mild.

There are also different subtypes of major depressive disorder depending on the symptoms and who gets them. For example, postpartum depression is often experienced by women who have recently given birth. Postpar-tum depression affects an estimated 10 to 15 percent of new mothers and can last for months in many cases, often subsiding thereafter only to recur with a new pregnancy. Another well-known form of depression is seasonal affective disorder (SAD), which seems to be linked to the time of the year when the symptoms develop. People typically develop SAD during autumn or winter, though their mood often improves in springtime. Research suggests that SAD may be due to the reduced sunlight during winter months. We will be talking more about postpartum depression and SAD later in the book.

For people with milder symptoms who don't quite meet the DSM cri-teria for major depression, there is another diagnosis that can be given:

dysthymic disorder, or persistent depressive disorder. While not as severe as major depressive disorder, dysthymic disorder can still be serious, with symptoms lasting for years before finally being recognized. These depressive symptoms can also cycle with periods of hypomanic moods (a condition referred to as cyclothymic disorder) or else lead to more severe depressive episodes (also known as double depression).

Whatever symptoms may develop, it is essential that sufferers seek medical help immediately to ensure that they receive the right treatment as soon as possible. Contrary to popular belief, depression doesn't just go away on its own.

3. What is the difference between being depressed and being unhappy?

Everyone experiences unhappiness at some point or the other in their lives and, as a result, people may *think* that they know what people with depression are going through. But anyone who has experienced both has no problem recognizing how different unhappiness and depression really are.

For people who are unhappy because of some problem or a recent setback or even when grieving the death of a loved one, it is still possible to find comfort in friends and family to ease the pain. In fact, there are a number of ways to cope with unhappiness, whether through the sympathy of people in our lives or simply by telling ourselves that "this too shall pass." And, sooner or later, the unhappiness does pass.

But for people suffering from depression, there are no easy fixes. Even though family and friends may offer emotional support, these symptoms don't disappear the way that unhappiness does. Because of what some researchers have termed the *prison of depression*, experiencing these symptoms often means feeling isolated from the rest of the world because other people simply can't understand what is happening. This sense of isolation makes depressed people feel as if an invisible wall is preventing them from experiencing any kind of relief.

And this wall often seems impossible to overcome. Not only do people who are depressed have difficulty describing what they are feeling to others but it can also prevent them from getting the help they need. Along with the sadness are a bevy of other emotions that also seem overwhelming: guilt, shame, and apathy, to name just a few—guilt, because depressed individuals can see how worried friends and family members are about them; shame, because they aren't able to handle life as well as everybody else (that other people have similar pains rarely makes a difference); and apathy, because of the belief that nothing they say or do can possibly change things for the better.

It's certainly possible for unhappiness to *become* depression if it goes on long enough or if the people experiencing it don't get the emotional support they need. For that matter, what we call unhappiness can vary widely across different cultures due to the kind of emotions that might be regarded as acceptable. This means that unhappiness may be regarded as more acceptable than depression since there is still a strong stigma against many mental disorders, which can often lead to individuals trying to keep their unhappiness hidden—something that can have major consequences for them in terms of their mental and physical health.

As we can see, while people can become unhappy for a variety of reasons, depression is much more severe and long lasting. For individuals who are particularly vulnerable to developing depression, whether due to problems in early childhood, heredity, or because of their life circumstances, unhappiness can certainly become depression if it goes on for longer than a few weeks. This is why anyone who is coping with feelings of unhappiness that don't seem to go away needs to talk to a qualified health professional as soon as possible. We will be getting into the different ways people can seek out help in the next section.

4. How widespread is depression?

As we can see from the previous question, depression can take many different forms, which makes it hard to estimate how common it really is. Still, recent statistics presented by the National Institute of Mental Health (NIMH) show that an estimated 16.2 million adults in the United States alone have had at least one major depressive episode in their lives. This represents about 6.78 percent of all adults aged eighteen or older. Of these, 10.3 million Americans will develop symptoms severe enough to be considered a serious impairment (4.3 percent of all adults).

Research looking at U.S. adolescents aged twelve to seventeen suggests that an estimated 3.1 million (12.8 percent) have had at least one major depressive episode. For females, in particular, the prevalence of major depression is even higher (19.4 percent compared to 6.4 percent for males). Of those adolescents with full-blown depression, 2.2 million of them will develop symptoms severe enough to leave them seriously impaired. This works out to 9 percent of the total population between the ages of twelve and seventeen.

Though these statistics apply to major depressive disorder alone, factoring in the prevalence rates for other mood disorders pushes the total number of people developing depressive symptoms even higher. When looking at bipolar disorder, for example, recent statistics by the NIMH indicate that 4.4 percent of all adults over the age of eighteen will experience bipolar disorder at some point in their lives. Of these, 2.8 percent had experienced at least one bipolar episode in the past year alone.

In many ways, however, these numbers are just the tip of the iceberg. Not only does major depression often go undiagnosed but many people may also develop severe symptoms that do not fit any particular diagnosis. According to the World Health Organization, there are more than three hundred million people around the world who suffer from depression, making it the leading cause of disability worldwide. In the United States alone, organizations such as the Depression and Bipolar Support Alliance estimate that depression affects twenty-three million Americans each year. That makes it the most common brain disease in the United States and one of the major contributors to long-term disability.

Despite there being effective treatments for depression, less than half of all sufferers of depression will receive any form of treatment. In the United States alone, 37 percent of adults with depression fail to get any form of treatment while only 44 percent received the full range of recommended treatment (with both psychotherapy and medication). An additional 6 percent only received medication with no additional treatment.

When looking at adolescents alone, these numbers seem even bleaker. According to U.S. statistics, 60 percent of depression sufferers between the ages of twelve and seventeen fail to get any form of treatment. Of those who do get treatment, only 19 percent receive both psychotherapy and medication. For the rest, almost all receive counseling alone, with only 2 percent receiving some form of medication.

In many developing nations that lack mental health resources, over 90 percent of people suffering from some form of depression will not receive any treatment. Though global health agencies are calling for more resources to help people suffering from depression and other mental health problems, the lack of trained health professionals and the stigma that surrounds mental illness in many countries still pose significant barriers for people in need.

And many mental health professionals suggest that cases of depression will continue to increase in future as more people come to accept that the symptoms they are experiencing may be a sign that they need professional help, which makes it more important than ever for people suffering from depression to reach out in any way they can to find the right treatment for themselves.

5. Who is most likely to develop depression?

While depression is something that can strike anyone at any time, researchers have identified different factors that may increase the risk of developing depression. Some of these factors will be explored in more detail later in the book; they include:

- Gender: In general, the risk of women developing major depression at some point in their lifetimes is around 20 percent compared to 10 percent for men. At this point, it isn't clear whether this can be due to biological differences or due to the fact that men are less likely than women to report emotional problems. Also, women tend to be more sensitive than men to the emotional pain resulting from relationship problems and are also more likely to seek treatment early when depressive symptoms develop.
- Age: Again, while depression can strike at any age, it appears most likely to affect people between the ages of 25 and 45 (with 32.5 being the average age). While late-life depression in people over the age of sixty-five also remains common, they are also less likely to seek treatment until their symptoms become much more severe. There can also be more difficulty in diagnosing depression in older adults since the symptoms may be confused with other medical conditions such as Alzheimer's disease, at least in the early stages.
- Family history: People with a family history of depression seem much more vulnerable to developing depression themselves. For someone with an identical twin suffering from depression, the likelihood of developing it as well is about 50 percent. For people who have a parent or sibling with depression, the risk of developing depression appears to be around 25 percent. It still isn't clear whether this is exclusively due to genetics or from growing up in a household with a depressed family member. Interestingly enough, even people who have an adopted family member with depression have an increased risk of developing the same symptoms themselves.
- Marital status: Though there are prominent exceptions, married people in general are less likely to develop depression than people who are either single or divorced. Also, the likelihood of depression rises sharply following divorce or the death of a spouse, often due to the grief that follows.
- Socioeconomic status: Not surprisingly, people who are unemployed, have an uncertain job situation, or are dealing with financial problems

are prone to depression. There also appears to be a link between depression and education, with people who are well educated being less likely to develop depression over time. Again, however, there are prominent exceptions, and the likelihood of depression often depends on how well people are able to cope with the financial and social problems in their lives.

- Ethnic background: For reasons that are still not clear, people from different ethnic backgrounds often vary in terms of whether they will develop depression at some point. This is often linked to differences in family support as well as the greater stigma concerning mental illness in some cultures. This stigma may make people from some ethnic groups less likely to admit to having emotional problems such as depression. As a result, the depression goes untreated and may become life threatening.

- Chronic health problems: People who suffer from chronic pain or other persistent medical conditions that affect the overall quality of their life often develop symptoms of depression that can make their recovery even harder. The relationship between pain and depression often leads to a vicious cycle, which can make coping much more difficult. Many people with chronic pain also develop problems with poor self-esteem and become pessimistic about their ability to move on with their lives.

- Being a victim: Whether it involves childhood physical or sexual abuse, being a target of bullying, or being a victim of violence, people who have been victimized are especially vulnerable to developing serious depression. This is usually linked to learned helplessness (i.e., losing confidence in our ability to take control of our life). We will explore this further later in the book.

As we can see, there are many different risk factors for depression. Even when these risk factors aren't causing the depression (such as with chronic pain), they can certainly make the depressive symptoms much worse. This is why treatment can be so important, both in terms of treating the depression itself as well as helping sufferers cope with the additional life problems.

6. How does depression change across the life span?

As people grow and mature over the years, the problems they face at each stage of life will change as well. In adolescents, for example, this means coming to terms with puberty and learning how to develop intimate relationships. As they grow older and become young adults, however, new problems will arise including the need to start careers, enter long-term romantic relationships, and take on new adult roles. As time passes, new responsibilities lead to new challenges, and it can also lead to problems with depression depending on how successfully these challenges are met.

While people can develop problems with depression at any age, the symptoms of depression that you experience will often change depending on the unique problems that you tend to face at these different stages of life.

Research looking at depression across the life span suggests that people may become more vulnerable at different stages in their life. Many of these studies have focused on factors that can lead to depression. These factors include loneliness, life satisfaction, and psychological well-being, and longitudinal studies reveal an interesting pattern, reflecting how we change and grow over time.

In one 2013 study looking at reported loneliness in over sixteen thousand adults ranging in age from eighteen to over one hundred, reported loneliness tended to peak around the age of thirty and decrease slowly until it started rising again when people were in their sixties and seventies. This basically means that loneliness (and depression) can occur at any age, though the reasons are often very different, depending on the particular stage in life. It also means that the methods we use to cope with loneliness and depression as adolescents or young adults aren't necessarily going to work as well when we are middle-aged or older.

And the depression we develop can be very different depending on the kind of life problems we are experiencing and where we are at a particular stage in life. For adults over the age of sixty-five, for example, the symptoms of geriatric depression, as it is known, can often be triggered by a growing sense of loneliness and often be confused with other medical problems such as dementia. While major depression appears to be much less common in seniors than it is in younger individuals (affecting as little as 1 percent according to recent studies), including other mood disorders raises the total number even higher (as much as 4 percent in women and 2.7 percent in men).

While these figures may not seem that alarming, the fact remains that people over the age of sixty-five represent the fastest growing population in the United States alone. In fact, one study suggests that two-thirds of all humans who have ever reached the age of sixty-five throughout history are still alive today. This means that the medical costs of dealing with new cases of geriatric depression may make it the most expensive medical condition to treat by 2025, if current trends continue.

Researchers looking at geriatric depression have also found that symptoms of depression are much more common in people over the age of seventy-five as they become more depressed due to developing other serious health problems.

7. What are some of the most common signs that someone is depressed?

Everyone is going to feel "the blues" at some point in their lives. Feelings of sadness or despondency are certainly common enough after experiencing a major loss or simply as part of the daily hassles we all go through. But, when these symptoms become overwhelming and refuse to go away, then things become more serious.

Even though depression is something that should only be diagnosed by a trained health professional (Dr. Google doesn't count), here are some common signs that might indicate that a person may be clinically depressed:

- Chronic fatigue, often to the point where it is difficult to get out of bed or take care of oneself.
- Persistent feelings of personal worthlessness, guilt, or helplessness. While we all experience occasional bouts of self-doubt, people who are depressed may find themselves being overwhelmed by these feelings.
- Feelings of pessimism and hopelessness.
- Sleep problems, including insomnia; disturbed sleep; or, in cases of severe depression, spending too much time sleeping.
- Concentration and memory problems. People who are depressed often find themselves unable to focus and often forget even trivial details.
- Loss of interest in activities that were once enjoyable. This can also involve an overall inability to feel pleasure (a condition known as anhedonia).
- Feelings of restlessness, whether due to racing thoughts that can't be controlled or due to a sense of muscular tension that make it difficult to get to sleep at night.
- Appetite problems, either eating too much or not eating at all.
- Irritability, or having a "short fuse"; this is a common symptom in people with depression.
- Persistent sad thoughts, usually linked to the feelings of pessimism and hopelessness already mentioned.
- Aches, pains, or headaches that don't seem to stop. These symptoms may not have a physical cause but can still seem very real to someone experiencing depression.

Not everyone experiencing depression is going to have all these symptoms, but they seem to be the most common ones. Again, however, nobody should try diagnosing themselves. People should seek medical attention immediately if they find these symptoms persisting for longer than a few days.

While there are no laboratory tests that can identify depression, medical doctors still need to conduct a thorough assessment to rule out other conditions that might be causing the symptoms. For example, in many people, conditions such as diabetes, hypothyroidism, and chronic fatigue syndrome can often produce symptoms that mimic depression. This is why doctors need to be cautious in the kind of diagnosis they make.

During the assessment, doctors may also ask questions about lifestyle, daily moods, and recent problems that could be triggering the symptoms as well as check on family history and past mental health problems. Some doctors may also want to try prescribing antidepressant medication, but the decision to take them should never be made lightly. Many antidepressants can have potential side effects, and nobody should take them without first educating themselves about whether or not medication is the best option available.

8. Are there other medical conditions that can mimic depression?

Though symptoms of depression seem unmistakable, there can be other medical issues that produce very similar symptoms. Here are just a few of the medical conditions that can be misdiagnosed as depression:

Hypothyroidism: This condition occurs when the thyroid gland isn't producing enough thyroid hormones. This can lead to significant health problems as well as symptoms such as fatigue, poor concentration, and a depressed mood. In the United States alone, there are as many as twenty million Americans with thyroid disease, but most of them have no idea of what is happening. Though there are key symptoms that can suggest thyroid problems to a doctor, many people with hypothyroidism may conclude that they are depressed instead. In most cases, a simple blood test can help clear up any misunderstanding, and a pill a day is all they may need.

Diabetes: Yes, people with undiagnosed type 2 diabetes can, and do, develop depression-like symptoms such as weight loss, fatigue, and increased irritability. Undiagnosed diabetes can also mean becoming more vulnerable to diabetes distress due to the often-exaggerated fears linked with diabetic symptoms, including dizziness, vertigo, and frequent hypoglycemic episodes. In many ways, the symptoms of this kind of distress are often hard to distinguish from actual depression, although, as with hypothyroidism, a medical examination and proper blood testing can ensure proper diagnosis and treatment.

Chronic fatigue syndrome (CFS): Also known as myalgic encephalomyelitis, this condition was, until fairly recently, routinely misdiagnosed as depression by medical doctors. Chronic fatigue symptoms can include concentration and sleep problems, extreme fatigue, and muscle pain. Since diagnostic testing for this condition is still limited, it is frequently underdiagnosed even today, and many CFS sufferers can be prescribed antidepressant medications. A similar condition, fibromyalgia, can also resemble depression, at least in the early stages. In fact, people suffering from either CFS or fibromyalgia often develop depression as well and may require treatment with antidepressant medication to help with their symptoms.

Symptoms resembling depression can also be linked to various problems associated with diet. This can include low blood sugar, vitamin deficiencies (particularly vitamin D), and dehydration, to name just a few possibilities. Even the withdrawal effects that can occur for people with different kinds of substance dependence, including caffeine, tobacco, and alcohol dependence, can often mimic depression.

There are also different cognitive disorders that can be misdiagnosed as depression. For example, while attention-deficit hyperactivity disorder (ADHD) is most often diagnosed in children, it can occur in adults as well. Since ADHD can produce symptoms such as insomnia, memory and concentration problems, and mood changes, many people developing these symptoms for the first time may assume they are depressed. For that matter, depression may often be misdiagnosed as dementia in older adults, as the symptoms can be very similar, at least in the early stages.

As I have already pointed out, it is essential that people not try diagnosing themselves when they are feeling depressed. There can be many different possible explanations for depression-like symptoms, and a wrong diagnosis can have serious consequences, in terms of delayed treatment.

9. What is learned helplessness?

Researchers have long recognized that laboratory animals kept caged away from other animals or otherwise enduring painful treatment that they cannot escape became passive and unresponsive. This has come to be known as learned helplessness and, due to the work of psychologists such as Martin Seligman, has become widely accepted as a way of understanding clinical depression and other types of mental illness.

According to the learned helplessness theory, people with depression become apathetic and despondent because they do not believe that they can control their own lives. In a sense, they have "given up" in much the same way that laboratory animals give up and become passive. Learned helplessness in people also means developing pathological symptoms such as disturbed sleep, inability to eat, ulcers, and other indicators of extreme stress, all of which are common signs of depression.

In one classic 1974 experiment on learned helplessness, human research subjects were split into three groups: members of the first group were exposed to a loud, unpleasant noise which could be stopped by pressing a button four times. The people in the second group were exposed to the same noise, but the button they were told would stop the noise did not work while there was no noise at all for the third group. In a second part of the experiment, subjects were then exposed to a loud noise in a room with a box that had a lever that could shut off the noise. Even though the lever worked, the subjects from the group who had previously been unable to control the noise made no attempt to push the lever while the subjects from the other conditions learned to turn off the noise very quickly. Essentially, the subjects from the not-in-control condition had learned to be helpless (even though they weren't).

In writing about learned helplessness and depression, Seligman himself argued that "the label 'depression' applies to passive individuals who believe they cannot do anything to relieve their suffering, who become depressed when they lose an important source of nurture . . . but it also applies to agitated patients who make many active responses, and who become depressed with no obvious external cause."

Studies looking at victims of domestic violence, childhood abuse, or frequent bullying have also shown that these victims often develop a sense of personal helplessness that make them less able to help themselves. This can result in passive behavior and emotional symptoms such as depression due to the belief that things are hopeless. Not surprisingly, victims often neglect their health and can experience weaker immune systems, slower recovery from injuries or illness, and a greater likelihood of medical problems such as heart disease.

Researchers have also identified parts of the brain that can play a critical role in both learned helplessness and depression. These can include the dorsal and ventral hippocampus, the prefrontal cortex, and other brain regions linked to the body's ability to cope with stress. Studies of biochemical markers of learned helplessness such as GABA and serotonin have also been invaluable in the development of new pharmaceutical treatments for depression.

While critics suggest that the learned helplessness theory only explains some symptoms of depression (such as apathy, feelings of hopelessness, lack of energy, and sadness), its value in developing more effective treatments for depression has been profound. These include techniques for building up self-esteem and helping people with depression overcome the belief that life is hopeless and can never become better. Cognitive behavioral techniques such as problem-solving therapy and learning to replace negative thinking with more positive ways of thinking have also become widely accepted in treating depression.

Though learned helplessness may only provide a partial answer to why people become depressed, it does highlight how important the need for control can be for those who require treatment. Being willing to take charge of their own lives and seeking help can be an essential part of building a healthier future.

10. How far back in history does depression go?

For as long as humans have been around, depression has likely existed as well. In fact, depression almost certainly existed long before there were any humans at all. As we can see from the section on learned helplessness, laboratory animals often display symptoms that resemble human depression in many ways, and this has been seen in animals living in the wild as well. Emotions such as grief and loss have been observed in all the different primate species and quite a few nonprimate species as well. Though we are in no position to ask these animals directly about their symptoms, animal models of depression have remained an important part of research into developing new and better ways of treating depressive symptoms.

Treatments for the symptoms of depression can be found in traditional medicine systems from around the world. Ancient Greek and Roman doctors frequently wrote about a condition called *melancholia* and similar essays on treating depression have also been written by doctors in ancient India and China. Even in the Middle Ages, the early Christian church fathers often wrote about a disease called *acedia* that could strike monks and nuns living isolated lives in desert monasteries (and which was often seen as being caused by laziness instead of depression).

In other cultures, healers often reported on symptoms very similar to what we would call depression in Western countries. In the highlands of Ecuador, for example, natives may develop what locals call *pena* whenever they experience a terrible loss. The symptoms of *pena* certainly seem familiar enough, including crying episodes, poor concentration, sleep and appetite problems, stomach and heart pains, and poor hygiene in severe cases. According to tradition, *pena* is due to a disturbance of the heart caused by being wronged by another person. While it is usually treated with herbal remedies, getting the accused person to make restitution appears to be part of the treatment process as well.

People living in different parts of Latin America can also report a condition known as *susto* (often called "soul loss") resulting from the soul leaving the body following a traumatic experience. Symptoms of *susto* can include insomnia, lethargy, diarrhea, lack of motivation, and nervousness. Largely seen as a spiritual illness, *susto* is usually treated by a visit from a spiritual healer who uses ritual cleansings and herbal teas to purge the sufferer of these symptoms.

Though healers and shamans have tackled the perennial problem of depression using whatever remedies they had available, they still had very different explanations for why people become depressed. The ancient Greeks blamed melancholia on an overabundance of black bile in the body while Chinese medicine blamed it on diseases of the liver. Avicenna, the Islamic physician whose writings on medicine would spread to Europe and beyond, believed that depression was caused by indigestion.

And, of course, there was always the old standby, demonic possession, which was often invoked to explain away symptoms of mental illness in men and (particularly) women. The fact that cases of mental patients being forced to undergo exorcisms occur even today says a lot about how popular the idea of depression having a supernatural cause can be.

Part of the problem in dealing with depression was that, for long stretches of history (and still today in many places), depression was regarded as being a spiritual and moral condition rather than a problem of the body. People who couldn't overcome depression on their own were often seen as too weak or too lazy to "get over" what was happening to them. This meant that people dealing with depression also had to cope with the shame of what was happening to them.

While our understanding of the causes of depression is much greater today, we are still dealing with many of the same issues relating to mental illness faced by our ancestors long ago. As we will see when we discuss how depression is viewed by different cultures, making real progress in how depressed people are treated and cared for remains a major challenge.

11. Why do so many people with depression try to hide their symptoms?

Along with the stigma attached to mental illness, there are numerous popular fallacies about depression, some of which have already been covered in the section on misconceptions.

Considering that everyone has episodes in which they feel down or unwanted, many people may not be too concerned when they begin experiencing symptoms of clinical depression. Not only might these symptoms not seem that severe at first but they may subside on their own after a while. It's only when the symptoms return or persist long enough to have a serious impact on life quality that people may realize that something is seriously wrong.

Even then, unfortunately, people are often afraid of telling friends or family about what they are going through. Along with the fear of being thought of as "crazy," there is also the sense of guilt that comes from being a burden to others. Whether the depression strikes a close family member, a friend, or a romantic partner, the stress of being a caregiver is going to make life harder and, not surprisingly, will make depressed people more despondent than ever.

There is also the fear of how medical doctors and other health professionals might respond to someone reporting feelings of depression. Along with the stigma surrounding psychiatric treatment, people may actively avoid seeking help due to the fear that it might get them "locked up" if they admit that they were having suicidal thoughts.

Another reason that people might want to conceal their symptoms is the belief that other people just won't understand what they are going through, something that is often a legitimate concern. Many people who discover that a child, a spouse, another family member, or even a close friend is suffering from depression often have no idea what to do about it. Most of us have only limited experience with mental illness aside from the various misconceptions we may have picked up from movies or television.

This either leads people to overreact and assume that their loved one is at immediate risk for suicide or a nervous breakdown or else to refuse to accept that the depression is a problem at all. Whether they try to cheer up the depressed person in the belief that this will cure their symptoms somehow or else urge them to go on antidepressant medication that might not be suitable for them, many people do not have the necessary facts to offer true help.

Sex differences may also be playing a role in whether or not people are willing to open up about their depression. While women seem more prone to depression overall, that may be due to men being far more likely than women to keep their symptoms hidden. Because of different sex roles, boys are encouraged control their emotions and to be strong and independent while girls are encouraged to show their emotions. As a result, admitting to feeling depressed can make many men feel unmanly, as they are no longer able to control their emotions. This can lead men dealing with depression to cope with its symptoms in other ways, including acting out aggressively or resorting to drugs and alcohol to numb the negative feelings. In extreme cases, depressed men may be more vulnerable to committing suicide.

Whether people are dealing with depression themselves or know someone else who is, it is vital to educate ourselves about depression, including its causes, effective treatments, and constructive ways of offering emotional support. Just showing depressed people that we are willing to do this on their behalf can often mean much to them and show them that we are ready and willing to help them recover.

Though the stigma surrounding depression is often very real, especially depending on where people happen to live, it is still important to be as open as possible about what they are experiencing. Not only does concealing symptoms mean delaying any possibility of getting help, but the stress of hiding depression often makes the problem much worse. And being willing to open up about what people are dealing with also allows family and friends to provide them with the kind of support they will need as well.

12. Is there a depression epidemic?

In recent years, depression has been increasingly recognized as a major public health issue worldwide. Not only are medical doctors around the world prescribing antidepressants in record numbers but more people than ever are opening up about being depressed. For this reason, the World Health Organization has launched a campaign aimed at improving mental health services around the world.

According to the latest Health of America report released by the Blue Cross Blue Shield Association, major depression diagnoses in the United States have soared between the years 2013 and 2016 alone. While there have been 33 percent more cases of major depression across all age groups, the highest rates have been found to be among adolescents (63 percent) and millennials (47 percent).

The actual diagnosis rates varied widely from state to state but forty-nine out of fifty states are reporting increases in depression (Hawaii being the only exception) with higher rates being found in the Northeast, Northwest, and the Midwest. Not surprisingly, women are being diagnosed with major depression at twice the rate as men though this will likely change too in future.

People diagnosed with major depression are also far less healthy in general than nondepressed individuals with 85 percent of all people with depression also having one or more serious health problems as well. This includes medical conditions such as heart disease; stroke; Parkinson's disease; and, in older people, a greater likelihood of developing dementia. This also leads to depressed people being more likely to rely on health care services with overall health care costs being more than double that of people without depression.

The increase in cases of adolescents with depression is especially startling because the rate of depression was very low in 2013 when these statistics were first collected (1.3 percent overall). Based on these results and other recent findings, the American Academy of Pediatrics has released new guidelines to screen all children and teenagers for depression to help catch these cases as early as possible. We will explore possible reasons for this rise in depression among young people later in the book.

Despite this apparent rise, however, some experts are disputing whether or not there is a real epidemic at work. In a controversial 2007 book, titled *The Loss of Sadness: How Psychiatry Transformed Normal Sorrow into Depressive Disorder*, authors Allan V. Horwitz and Jerome C. Wakefield argue that the apparent rise in new cases of depression in recent years may just be an illusion. While they acknowledge that depression is certainly real, Horwitz and Wakefield suggest that the actual number of people experiencing depression is no greater than it has ever been.

As for why new cases are being diagnosed, the authors suggest that more people are seeking treatment because of the increased publicity surrounding depression in the popular media. Not only are we seeing many more news stories about depression, including stories about celebrities dealing with mood problems but we are also seeing more movies and television programs featuring characters with depression—something that was much rarer even twenty years ago.

At the same time, the psychiatric profession has introduced new ways of defining depression that makes even ordinary cases of sadness seem to be something that needs medical treatment. As well, medical doctors are prescribing antidepressant medication much more frequently than they ever did before, and even the popular media helps this trend with stories about the positive benefits of medications such as Prozac (and it likely helps that pharmaceutical companies are now advertising antidepressants in popular magazines and websites. Along with encouraging people who might otherwise let their depression go untreated to seek help, many patients may be asking their doctors for medication to help them deal with problems they used to resolve on their own.

Whatever the reasons for this new depression epidemic that seems to be occurring, or whether this increase will continue in future, it is more important than ever that people who develop symptoms of depression reach out to get the help they need. There is less excuse than ever to suffer in silence.

Causes and Risk Factors

13. Why do individuals become depressed?

As we have already seen in the Introduction, depression seems virtually universal and has even been seen in many nonhuman species. In fact, just about any pet owner or animal breeder can tell stories about the deep emotions that animals seem to experience, including depression and grief following the death of a loved one. Along with the learned helplessness often seen in animals kept in cages, especially when isolated or deprived of normal social stimulation, researchers studying animals in the wild have recorded numerous instances of grief and despondency in many animals, suggesting that these are truly universal traits. Certainly, photographs showing elephant calves grieving for mothers who have been killed by poachers demonstrate how real this emotion can be.

Researchers have identified numerous different causes for depression, ranging from genetic and biochemical factors to psychological causes, including the influence of stress, trauma, life changes, and even the amount of sunlight we happen to be getting. We will be exploring all these different factors later in the book.

But can we understand more about why we become depressed by looking at possible clues from our evolutionary history? Some researchers have suggested that we can. For example, one proposed explanation is the "behavioral shutdown" hypothesis. This suggests that depression can actually be a healthy coping mechanism under some circumstances, as it helps us adapt to extreme situations by reducing activity as much as possible.

In other words, being depressed leads us to take time out of our lives to recover and regain the inner resources needed to cope in future. Being in a depressed state can also force us to ruminate about our lives and give us the time needed to make effective changes. Our ability to survive depression also depends on the support we receive from family and friends, something often seen with animals living in social colonies in the wild as well.

There is also the "psychic pain" hypothesis which suggests that the kind of emotional distress seen in depression is very similar to how physical pain affects the body. For example, the physical pain we experience after being burned forces us to withdraw from the fire to prevent being injured further. In much the same way, the psychic pain that can lead to depression can also act as a warning that certain activities may harm us if we are not careful.

According to brain imaging research supporting the psychic pain hypothesis, depressed people show greater activation of those brain regions that have also been linked to pain perception. Many of the symptoms found in depression, including disrupted sleeping and eating patterns, loss of pleasure, and impaired motor functioning, are also found in chronic pain patients. While severe depression can be viewed as a more extreme form of responding to psychic pain, mild depression can be an effective strategy under the right circumstances.

Though trying to explain different forms of mental illness in terms of evolution is still controversial, the possible role of depression as a way of adapting to stress can help us understand why it appears so universal. It may also help explain why depression can often take different forms, depending on the kind of life circumstances people may face, the inner resources they have available to them, and the help they can receive from the family members and friends who care for them.

14. Is depression linked to trauma?

It's hardly surprising that people who survive a traumatic experience are often going to develop posttraumatic symptoms afterward. As we have seen in Question 8, many people affected by natural or man-made disasters may lose confidence in their ability to cope effectively. Whether this traumatic event is something that happens only once (such as a natural disaster) or repeatedly (such as with victims of domestic abuse), the despair that can occur due to this belief in their own helplessness can be extremely hard to overcome. And as new traumatic events occur, this sense of helplessness becomes progressively worse.

But this kind of learned helplessness doesn't just affect people who are directly exposed to traumatic events. Family members or friends of trauma victims can also experience these symptoms when they hear about these first-hand experiences and try to provide emotional support. This is known as secondary traumatic stress, and it can take a toll as well.

Research studies have long shown that children of Holocaust victims often develop trauma symptoms as well from hearing the stories of their parents or from grandparents describing what had happened to them. Even health professionals who deal with trauma patients can develop secondary trauma due to repeatedly listening to their patients' experiences. Though this secondary trauma may not seem as serious as what trauma victims experience directly, it can still have an impact that shapes how people view their own lives and how they deal with stress. And, as you can imagine, this is one of the reasons that the suicide rate in health care professionals can be so much higher than average.

But there is also the depression that can occur in people who experience long-term trauma. People living in war zones, who are in long-term abusive relationships, or are dealing with chronic sexual or physical abuse often develop what has been termed *complex posttraumatic disorder* (C-PTSD). First proposed by Judith Herman in her 1992 book, *Trauma and Recovery*, she suggested that people dealing with long-term stress often showed symptoms very different from people experiencing single-event traumas.

As a result, they can often become passive and withdrawn (due to learned helplessness), or develop highly unstable personalities. Along with all the classic symptoms of depression, they can also show other symptoms such as self-cutting; substance abuse; violent behavior; and, in many cases, suicide attempts.

This kind of chronic trauma can take many different forms though. Religious, sexual, or ethnic minorities in many Western countries are often victimized by violent hate crimes intended to intimidate them. Whether or not individual members experience these crimes directly, the fact that the violence was directed at the community to which they belong is enough to make them feel victimized. This is often referred to as identity trauma since it involves attacks on a person's sense of identity as much as it is a physical threat. There is also collective trauma, which can strike an entire nation after a wide-scale event such as 9/11 or the recent Boston Marathon bombings. Though the panic subsides fairly quickly, the ever-present sense of *Will it happen again?* never really goes away.

As you can see, trauma can occur in many different ways and often affects not only victims of trauma but the people close to them as well. This is why counseling can be so important for health care professionals and even family members trying to take care of loved ones in need.

15. Why is depression so common in young people?

For reasons that are still unclear, young people seem to be particularly vulnerable to depression. According to statistics released by the National Institute of Mental Health (NIMH) in 2015, 12.5 percent of adolescents aged from twelve to seventeen have had at least one major depressive episode. Even more alarmingly, these figures seem to be part of a rising trend, with the percentage of young people dealing with depression showing a sharp rise over the past ten years.

Research has also shown that adolescents who develop symptoms of depression at an early age (age thirteen or younger) are more likely to experience chronic depression as they grow older. In one study looking at adolescent depression, 35 percent of boys and girls who had significant depressive symptoms at age thirteen showed similar problems at age seventeen. Girls showed greater levels of depression overall, and boys suffering from depression showed little improvement with time.

While there have been different explanations giving for the rising problem of depression in young people, one recent research study is suggesting that the rise of new technology, including smartphones and the Internet, may be playing a role. The study, which examined trends in emotional well-being in adolescents from 1991 to 2016, shows a significant drop in personal happiness beginning in 2012. Breaking these results down further, researchers found that adolescents who spent much of their time with electronic media (smartphones, electronic games, and the Internet) were generally less happy, were less satisfied with their lives, and had lower self-esteem than their less connected counterparts.

Among the possible reasons for the depression-technology link are the general drop in face-to-face social interactions among adolescents seen in recent years, the loss in sleep time often related to excessive screen use, and potential addiction issues due to becoming too dependent on social media. There are also the mental health issues that can arise from cyber-bullying or other forms of electronic harassment, which can also influence self-esteem and psychological well-being.

As vulnerable as young people in general appear to be, girls are twice as likely to be diagnosed with a mood disorder as boys. Along with differences in brain development, girls also go through the physical changes linked to puberty around two years earlier than boys. This makes them especially vulnerable to the effect of social influences, including cyberbullying and peer pressure relating to personal appearance. It's probably not surprising that girls are far more likely to spend time on social media sites than boys.

This leads to increased exposure to negative media influences, including images of "ideal" females who often make them feel inadequate as a result. They are also prone to "body shaming" if they fail to meet these often unrealistic beauty standards, which can also lead to rejection from other young people their same age.

So, what are the long-term consequences of adolescent depression? Studies seeking to answer this question have shown that adolescents suffering from depression were substantially more likely to develop depression as adults (aged twenty-one or over). They were also more vulnerable to developing anxiety problems when older though available evidence is mixed on whether adolescent depression in linked to increased risk of suicide as adults.

As you can see, adolescents suffering from depression need to begin treatment as soon as possible to avoid the serious problems that can develop otherwise. Studies examining different treatment approaches have been shown to be effective in relieving symptoms of depression. Along with medication to control depressive symptoms, supportive counseling can also be used to teach coping skills and help adolescent patients understand what is happening to them. While cognitive behavioral therapy remains the gold standard in treating adolescent depression due to the numerous studies that have attested to its effectiveness, we have also seen a rise in newer treatment methods that can also help.

Along with new treatment approaches such as dialectical behavior therapy and short-term psychodynamic therapy, therapists have also had success with a range of other treatment approaches such as art and music therapy. Family counseling is also available, which allows adolescent patients to attend counseling with a parent or other family members to help improve communication and cope better with stress. Young people considering supportive counseling usually have the option of either individual therapy or joining a treatment group in which group members support each other and encourage social skills that can make depression easier to control. We will be discussing treatment programming in more detail in a later section.

Aside from more traditional treatment approaches, school-based psychosocial programs have become more common in recent years to provide mental health care for children and adolescents who might otherwise "slip between the cracks." While most of these programs focus on issues such as substance abuse and suicide, they also provide information on depression and coping to help students recognize the symptoms they might be experiencing.

One example of a program with proven effectiveness in curbing suicide and depression was developed by the Cincinnati Children's Hospital Medical Center for use in high schools throughout the Cincinnati area. The program, titled *Surviving the Teens*, provides information on teen stressors, coping strategies, and warning signs of depression and suicide. Research on the more than sixty thousand high school students who have already gone through the program has shown a significant drop in suicide attempts as well as reduced social anxiety and depressive symptoms.

While programs such as *Surviving the Teens* are still in the experimental stage, treatment resources for young people dealing with depression can be found in most places. There are also online resources for young people who might be reluctant to talk about their problems in person. Check the Appendix section for more information about programs in your area.

16. What causes postpartum depression?

While cases of mothers killing their children due to postpartum psychiatric problems are mercifully rare, well-known examples reported in the news have made us more aware of how vulnerable some women can be to problems such as depression after giving birth. Up until relatively recently, however, women have been afraid to talk about their postpartum symptoms for fear of being thought of as crazy or that they might pose a danger to their children. This often leads to needless suffering and a sense of shame that might prevent women from seeking help until it is too late in many cases.

In reality, postpartum or postnatal depression affects around 15 percent of new mothers and can also affect new fathers as well. Symptoms of postpartum depression can include:

- Persistent sadness or a sense of feeling "empty"
- Feelings of hopelessness or helplessness
- Mood swings
- A sense of worthlessness or poor self-esteem
- Exhaustion
- Difficulty bonding with the baby
- Lacking confidence in maternal or paternal instincts

Many other familiar symptoms of depression also appear including loss of libido, appetite changes, lack of energy, loss of interest in activities that used to be enjoyed, social withdrawal, and insomnia. People suffering from postpartum depression can also develop cognitive problems such as poor concentration, impaired decision-making ability, and distractibility. Persistent worries can develop, including an overwhelming fear of becoming violent or suicidal. Along with worrying about possibly harming their children, people with postpartum depression may also worrying about injuring a spouse or other family member, or even committing suicide.

While postpartum depression can become life threatening if the symptoms persist long enough, there is also a more severe form known as postpartum psychosis. This means, along with symptoms of depression, sufferers can also develop psychotic symptoms such as visual or auditory hallucinations (i.e., hearing voices ordering them to kill their baby or commit some other violent act), delusions, or grossly distorted thinking patterns. While postpartum psychosis is relatively rare (occurring in about one out of every thousand pregnancies), it can be especially dangerous, as it can often appear even in women with no prior history of mental health problems.

Still, there can be warning signs that might indicate that some women are at risk for postpartum depression. One of the strongest of these is prenatal depression, which can occur in 7 to 20 percent of all pregnancies. Symptoms for prenatal depression are very similar to those seen in postpartum depression and can be triggered by pregnancy stress, relationship problems, financial worries, medical complications, or trauma.

There are also milder forms of postpartum depression such as the "baby blues," which occurs in 80 percent of all pregnancies and usually goes away on its own after a week or two. While women who experience baby blues may be at risk of developing more severe postpartum depression in future pregnancies, the symptoms are usually not that severe in themselves so long as they don't last longer than a couple of weeks.

While the American College of Obstetricians and Gynecologists recommends that all women be screened for symptoms of depression during pregnancy and in the months following birth, this often doesn't happen unless the women themselves report problems. Though universal screening for depression is happening in some places, including parts of Canada, many other jurisdictions have been slow to follow suit.

As we come to understand more about prenatal and postpartum depression, better treatment options are becoming available. But not all women suffering from symptoms of depression linked to pregnancy are willing to admit what they are feeling and are delaying treatment as a result. If you are dealing with prenatal/postpartum depression, or if someone close to you is, don't hesitate to discuss these symptoms with a health care professional as soon as possible.

17. What causes seasonal affective disorder?

While many people experience the "blues" during the autumn and winter months, the different ways that our bodies change from one season to the next can be profound. Even though you might not be aware of it, your mood and behavior often change depending on where you are living as well as the amount of sunlight you take in on a daily basis. For example, many people living in northern countries often report feeling much more depressed and apathetic during winter months, something that is much less common in people living in more southern climates.

Back in the 1980s, medical researcher Norman E. Rosenthal and his colleagues at the NIMH first identified a condition he referred to as seasonal affective disorder (SAD). In his 1993 book, *Seasons of the Mind*, Dr. Rosenthal suggested that the seasonal changes in depression experienced by him and many others were likely linked to not getting enough sunlight in winter months. Symptoms of SAD are very similar to those of other mood disorders: sadness, lethargy, appetite and sleep changes, and a difficulty waking up in the morning.

Women and children are far more likely to experience these symptoms and, as expected, they are much more common in northern latitudes than in places closer to the equator. People with SAD also report sleeping more hours during winter months than they do during the summer (as much as two or three hours longer in many cases). Also, for reasons that are still unclear, SAD symptoms are most apparent around the age of twenty-seven and decrease over time as people grow older.

Though not formally listed in the DSM as a distinct mood disorder, people are considered to be suffering from SAD if their depression has a clear seasonal pattern (more severe at some times of the year than others) and last for two years or more. While it's hard to say how common SAD really is, Rosenthal reported in his book that fourteen million American suffer from SAD while another fourteen million suffer from a milder form known as the "winter blues."

Studies looking at the physiology of SAD suggest that symptoms are related to the circadian rhythms that are found in all living organisms. These are the day-night rhythms that regulate our sleeping and waking periods and which are controlled by the master biological clock located in the supra-chiasmic nucleus (SCN) of the brain's hypothalamus. This master clock is directly affected by light and darkness due to the neurological pathway linking ganglion cells in the retinas to the SCN. As these retinal ganglion cells are activated by optimum light levels, the SCN triggers the brain's pineal gland to suppress the production of melatonin.

Melatonin is a specialized hormone produced by the pineal gland that cues the body to prepare for sleep. Over the course of the average day, melatonin levels remain low and only rise in the evening to prepare the body for sleep. We become drowsier and less alert, and most of our normal physical processes begin to shut down. Over the next twelve hours, melatonin levels remain high until exposure to increasing light returns them to daytime lows.

While our bodies evolved to the natural day-night light cycle, artificial lighting and electronic devices have had a serious disruptive effect on this cycle over the past two generations. Add to that our dependence on electronic devices such as cell phones and computers, and it hardly becomes surprising that young people in particular have become much more prone to insomnia and related problems such as SAD.

For people suffering from SAD symptoms, there are a range of potential treatments that can be effective. One of the most well known of these treatments is light therapy (also known as phototherapy). This basically involves the use of a bright light to simulate natural outdoor light during the first hour of waking up each day. For people suffering from fall-onset SAD, regular use of light therapy can relieve symptoms after just a few days in many cases. While light therapy devices can be purchased online, it is essential to get proper medical advice to avoid buying one of the many low-quality devices that are often advertised.

While light therapy isn't the right solution for everyone, there are also medications that can help, though it can often take weeks before the medication takes effect. People who want to try medication to handle SAD symptoms should be aware of possible side effects as well as the possibility that they may have to try different medications before finding one that works.

Anyone who thinks they might be suffering from SAD should see their family doctor to investigate their symptoms and to discuss the different treatment options available. While there are any number of websites offering treatments and promising quick relief, much like other kinds of depression, nobody should try diagnosing and treating themselves by relying on Dr. Google. No matter how distressing symptoms can be, it is essential to make the right choices when looking for help.

18. Is depression caused by a brain disorder?

While we are still learning about all the complex processes that allow our brains to function the way they do, numerous research studies have already linked different forms of depression to biochemical and anatomical changes in the brain. For example, key neurotransmitters such as serotonin, noradrenaline, and dopamine help the brain regulate biological processes through the body as well as in those regions of the brain controlling different emotions such as fear and anger.

Serotonin, in particular, helps control mood, appetite, and sleep, and researchers have long known that reduced serotonin levels in key brain regions result in clinical symptoms of depression. This has led to what researchers refer to as the serotonin model of depression and has inspired the development of numerous antidepressant drugs that work by reinforcing serotonin activity in different ways.

While the role that dopamine and noradrenaline play in depression are not as well understood, new research suggests that all three neurotransmitters can contribute to different symptoms of depression. It also suggests that new medications can be developed that can treat cases of depression that don't respond to medications that work on serotonin levels alone.

But researchers have also identified other biological markers linked to depression, though it is still unclear what role they are playing in mood disorders. For example, cortisol, produced in the adrenal glands, is a critical part of the body's resistance to stress and trauma. People experiencing the usual "fight or flight" reaction to stress are more prone to exhaustion afterward and may also be vulnerable to depression as their cortisol levels, and often their serotonin levels, drop below normal.

Ironically enough, even positive stressful events such as the birth of a new baby or a wedding can have the same effect on the body's cortisol levels. As you can see in the section on postpartum depression, new mothers can be particularly vulnerable to symptoms of depression though, in most cases, they tend not to be that serious.

For that matter, chronic depression itself could become a stressor given the mental strain involved in trying to cope. The nervous system becomes overstimulated with the stress of coping, and this is followed by the exhaustion stage as the body tries to recover. Not surprisingly, many people suffering from depressive episodes can report feeling exhausted, though, given that their original depression is still there, they often become despondent as well as lose hope of getting better.

Research also shows that depressed people often have significantly elevated levels of cortisol in their bloodstreams. The greater the emotional distress, the higher the cortisol levels become as well, not to mention other hormones linked to stress.

But studies have also found significant differences in brain structure between people with severe depression and control subjects. For example, people suffering from depression appear to have a hippocampus that is 15 percent smaller than in people without depression. The amygdala is also much larger than normal. Both the hippocampus and amygdala are critical components of the brain's limbic system, which regulates our ability to regulate emotion.

While these results may also be the result of stress (e.g., the amygdala also regulates cortisol levels), the link between brain anatomy and depression seems to be very real. Other brain differences linked to depression include abnormally small neurons and fewer glial cells in the brain's prefrontal cortex; research, though, is still ongoing.

Despite all the research showing biological markers linked to depression, the question of cause and effect still hasn't been answered. Are these different biological factors causing the depression or are they the result of *being* depressed? And then there is the potential impact of stress on the body, which is still being explored. The changes in the brain's biochemistry and anatomy that have been associated with depression may actually be caused by how our bodies cope with stress.

At this point, it appears safe to say that depression is an extremely complex disorder that can be linked to both psychological and biological factors. As we have seen in previous sections, people may become vulnerable to depression for various reasons, including family history, early childhood problems, trauma, or life problems. Understanding these different causal factors and what can make people more susceptible to becoming depressed will be critical in finding better ways to prevent depression and to treat the symptoms as they develop.

19. Is depression genetic?

Despite numerous studies looking at the biology of depression, the question of whether depression is caused by heredity or the environment continues to be controversial. Still, research with identical twins and adoptees, as well as family studies of people with depression, does suggest that the risk of depression is higher for those with a close relative who suffers from depression.

For example, having an identical twin with depression places people at a much higher risk of developing depression themselves than they would with a depressed fraternal twin (due to greater genetic similarity). To rule out the possible effects of family upbringing, some researchers have also looked at identical twins who were separated as infants and raised in separate families, though, so far, the sample sizes have tended to be too small to make for any conclusive results.

Even having a close family member with depression (such as a parent or sibling) may mean a greater chance of developing similar symptoms over time. One classic study looking at psychiatric patients diagnosed with different types of depression found that 22.9 percent of the mothers of these patients and 13.6 percent of the fathers had mood disorders as well. As for their siblings, the risk of them also having depression was substantially higher when one or both of their parents also had symptoms.

Many of the research studies looking at genetic factors in bipolar and unipolar depression have focused on the heritability estimate of these different conditions. Heritability is defined as the proportion of total variation between individuals that can be accounted for by genetic differences alone—in other words, the extent to which a trait is caused by genetic rather than environmental factors. Even though heritability estimates have varied widely across different research studies, one 2006 overview of twin research places the heritability of depression at around 38 percent (suggesting a moderately strong genetic component).

Despite the extensive research done on the heritability of depression in humans, no specific genetic markers for depression have been clearly identified. Given the difficulty of doing this kind of research in humans, most studies to date have used laboratory animals specially bred to mimic different symptoms of depression. These symptoms can include reduced appetite, anxious behavior, vulnerability to learned helplessness, and an inability to feel pleasure. There are also laboratory procedures used to simulate depression in laboratory animals and to measure the effectiveness of new antidepressant medications.

While results have been largely inconsistent, some potential candidates for depression marker genes have been identified using animal research. Studies are still underway to determine how these specific genes may interact with environmental factors to increase the risk of depression as well as how they relate to stress and coping.

Even though most evidence to date shows that genetic factors can play a role in the development of depression, it is important to remember how complex depression can be. As we have seen so far in this book, people can become depressed for numerous reasons. For that reason, no two cases of depression are alike, and there is no way to predict the kind of symptoms people will develop and how well they will respond to treatment.

Much more research will be needed before we can develop a real understanding about how genetics and environmental factors can interact to make people more vulnerable to depression.

20. Can bullying lead to depression?

Bullying is typically defined as the use of force, threats, or coercion to abuse or dominate others. In recent years, researchers have identified four main types of bullying:

- emotional or relational bullying aimed at undermining a victim's social reputation, often by spreading rumors about their behavior (sexual or otherwise)
- verbal bullying involving the use of name calling, teasing or mocking, or other verbal abuse aimed at undermining self-confidence or isolating intended victims from their support networks
- physical bullying, or the use of force, stealing possessions, or vandalism to intimidate victims. Physical bullying usually escalates over time and often involves groups of abusers singling out individuals they consider to be vulnerable.
- cyberbullying is the newest form of bullying and was made possible by the rise of digital communication devices and an Internet allowing for anonymous posting of messages, images, and videos. Just like emotional bullying, cyberbullying often involves undermining a victim's social reputation by spreading rumors as well as posting graphic images taken without the victim's consent. Along with harassment, victims can also be stalked by anonymous abusers as a prelude to physical or sexual violence later.

Though cyberbullying has become especially prominent over the past few years due to our growing dependence on social media, most bullies will use more than one form of intimidation on their victims.

While most commonly associated with school-age victims, bullying can occur just about anywhere, including in work settings, prisons, military bases, and so on. Since many victims of bullying often have difficulty proving what is happening, filing a report with school authorities or police often fails to stop the harassment. This can lead to significant emotional problems for most bullying victims due to the sense of helplessness and paranoia that can develop with time. Cases of victims committing suicide or developing serious mental health issues or substance abuse issues are hardly uncommon.

The role that bullying can play in the mental health of adolescents is especially serious, as it often occurs at a time when young people are still developing their own sense of self-esteem and social competence. Undermining this self-esteem and isolating victims from the support of friends or family often leads to a sense of helplessness; social anxiety; and, in many cases, a "no way out" mentality.

Research studies examining the effects of chronic bullying on adolescents have consistently shown that all forms of bullying can lead to increased risk of depression as well as suicidal thoughts and attempts. Young people bullied in school are also prone to academic problems as well as have a greater likelihood of dropping out of school to escape harassment. Though most research to date has focused on verbal and physical bullying, high-profile news stories of adolescents committing suicide due to cyberbullying have demonstrated the kind of impact it can have.

But bullying doesn't just lead to psychological problems for victims. Recent studies looking at the role of bullying on physical health have shown that victimized young people are at risk for problems such as insomnia, headaches, gastrointestinal problems (including ulcers), and respiratory problems. This is largely due to the impact of stress, which can lead to a compromised immune system, hypertension, greater production of stomach acid, and other health issues.

A 2017 study looking at over eleven thousand European adolescents reported an overall prevalence rate of 9.2 percent for physical bullying, 36.1 percent for verbal bullying, and 33.0 percent for relational bullying. While victims of physical bullying are at the highest risk for suicide, any bullying victim should be considered at risk for suicide. This is especially true if they are dealing with other problems such as depression or a perceived lack of support from parents. There were also gender differences in the kind of bullying experienced (boys were more likely to be physically bullied while girls were more prone to relational bullying).

As for the long-term effects of chronic bullying, many adults who reported being bullied when younger reported symptoms that persisted well into adulthood. Not only are victims of chronic bullying more prone to mental health problems such as depression and social anxiety, but they can require treatment to deal with posttraumatic stress as well.

Not only is bullying a pervasive problem among young people in particular, but the rise of the Internet and popularity of digital communication tools has provided bullies with even more tools to use in targeting victims. Since cyberbullying is usually anonymous, seeking legal protections against this kind of harassment is often difficult.

While bullying prevention programs are becoming more widely used in schools and other venues where bullying problems have been reported, many victims still prefer not to come forward due to fear of not being believed or possible retaliation. This often leaves the victim with no recourse except to suffer in silence or find some way of escape. Escape usually manifests through dropping out of school completely or else through negative coping strategies such as substance abuse, violent response, or suicidal behavior.

There are resources available for victims of bullying and their families, both in terms of working to stop the abuse as well as in dealing with the psychological consequences. The appendix provides information on national organizations that can refer bullying victims to local treatment services.

21. How is grief related to depression?

Anyone who has ever experienced the loss of a close family member or friend is going to find themselves dealing with grief. While the usual symptoms of grief are going to resemble depression in many ways (including feelings of restlessness, appetite changes, sleep difficulties, concentration problems, etc.), there are important differences as well.

Though not everyone is going to grieve in the same way, working through the emotional turmoil of grief is a healthy way to come to terms with this kind of loss. Still, sooner or later, the grieving process usually comes to an end. While there is no fixed time period associated with grief, symptoms usually subside after a year or so as we learn to move on with our lives. Though we can still feel the loss on anniversary dates, for example, this grief is usually manageable and temporary.

For some people, however, the symptoms of grief can persist much longer than usual. They may also find themselves experiencing symptoms that are much more intense than what is typically seen in normal grief. These symptoms often include an inability to focus on anything other than the death of the loved one, emotional numbness, a sense that life has lost its purpose, and a sense of personal blame (such as believing that they could have prevented the death somehow). People showing these symptoms are often diagnosed as suffering from complicated grief.

While not formally recognized as a mental disorder in the latest version of the DSM-V, complicated grief appears most likely to occur in females, particularly older females, following a traumatic loss, such as the unexpected or violent death of a loved one. A previous history of mental health problems, including depression or PTSD, can also make people more vulnerable, especially if they are socially isolated and lack a strong support network of friends and family. In extreme cases, people dealing with complicated grief may also develop psychotic symptoms, including hallucinations of a loved one's voice or image, as well as distorted thinking and delusional beliefs.

Since the symptoms of complicated grief are so similar to major depression, diagnosis and treatment should only be carried out by qualified medical professionals. Also, considering that people with complicated grief are often at risk for suicide, substance abuse, or other negative coping strategies, cases of suspected complicated grief need to be carefully monitored for their own safety. While bereavement counseling can often be useful in dealing with grief, more severe mental health problems will often require treatment with medication as well as supportive counseling to help control grief symptoms.

If left untreated, the symptoms of complicated grief will often lead to serious mental health problems as well as medical issues resulting from chronic stress and increased risk of suicide or substance abuse. The stress of prolonged grief can also lead to a wide range of physical ailments, including heart disease, a reduced immune system, increased risk of stroke, and dementia.

For people dealing with grief symptoms that don't seem to be going away, it is essential that they see their family doctors to determine what kind of treatment they might need. Along with medications that might help, there are also specialized cognitive behavioral therapy programs that have been developed for people dealing with this kind of grief.

22. Is depression linked to early childhood problems?

As we have already seen, people who have experienced childhood abuse, whether physical, sexual, or emotional, are going to have an increased risk of developing depression later in life. But this isn't simply due to the effect of trauma but also because of the very nature of the emotional bond that forms between parents and their children during the first few years of life.

Psychologists have long known that children raised in impersonal institutions such as orphanages are at a much higher risk of developing mental health problems. According to psychiatrist John Bowlby and other researchers, children are born with a biological need to form strong attachments as a way of surviving. The first attachment children develop is toward their mother (or some other primary caregiver) who supplies all their biological needs during infancy and early childhood.

According to attachment theory, there is a critical period between infancy and the age of five when a strong attachment needs to form to allow for healthy emotional development. If that attachment fails to form or is disrupted for any reason, children will develop behavioral and emotional problems that will get even worse with time.

As part of her own research with children, psychologist Mary Ainsworth identified four attachment styles that can result from how children interact with parents during those first few years:

- Secure attachment. This is the attachment style most likely to lead to healthy emotional development as children become adults. They also represent the majority of the children Ainsworth studied. These are the children who are confident in their relationship with an attachment figure (usually the mother) who is sensitive to their needs. Because of this secure attachment, children are less afraid and more curious about the world around them.
- Insecure avoidant. In some children, lacking a normal attachment can result in a more independent attachment style including reduced stranger anxiety and lack of distress when the mother/caregiver leaves. This attachment style often results from a caregiver who is emotionally distant and who does not attend to the child's needs.
- Insecure resistant/ambivalent. Due to inconsistent care during the first few years of life, children may become more clingy but also reject the caregiver when they attempt to interact with them. Also, these children have no sense of security from their caregiver and can be difficult to soothe as a result.
- Fearful avoidant. Children who have experienced significant trauma early in life may develop an inability to trust others and avoid any kind of emotional closeness. Not only do they avoid emotional attachments, but they may also feel they are unworthy.

As children grow older, these early attachment styles can play an important role in their later emotional and social development, not to mention the kind of mental health problems that they can develop as they become adults. For example, research studies have shown that adults with a history of insecure attachments are much more prone to developing depression than secure individuals. They are also much more prone to relationship problems, have lower self-esteem, sleep problems, are more prone to serious health problems, and have greater difficulty managing emotions.

Most of the treatment programs for helping with attachment issues as well as mental health problems have been developed for adolescents in particular. Such programs focus on helping adolescents overcome problems of early childhood and develop into successful adults. For adults dealing with long-term attachment problems along with depression or other mental health problems, treatment is usually much more intensive than for adolescents and can take much longer as a result.

There are few research studies looking into how successful adult treatment can be. All that can really be said is that the impact of early childhood attachment problems can last a lifetime in many cases. This is why it is essential for adolescents dealing with relationship problems to get proper counseling as soon as possible.

23. Is chronic pain linked to depression?

Chronic pain remains one of the most vexing medical problems facing us today—usually defined as persistent pain that lasts six months or longer, chronic pain can strike people of all ages. While estimates vary widely around the world, most surveys suggest that anywhere from 10 to 55 percent of all adults are going to report chronic pain problems at some point in their lives. In the United States alone, nearly half of all Americans suffer from one or more chronic conditions that can produce the kind of aches and pains that seriously undermine quality of life.

And the costs of dealing with chronic pain are often astronomical. In the United States alone, the annual cost for society runs to about $125 billion annually in terms of health care services, disability payments, time lost from work, and lost taxes. But this doesn't even take into consideration how chronic pain can affect people, both mentally and physically.

Along with familiar culprits such as arthritis, bursitis, fibromyalgia, gout, and stomach ulcers, people can also experience persistent pain from gallbladder disease, cancer, and multiple sclerosis to name just a few potential causes. But pain can also result from lifestyle issues such as poor posture, obesity, injuries from accidents, poor working conditions, and even simple repetitive movements that can lead to carpal tunnel syndrome, rotator cuff problems, joint aches, and so on.

For that matter, many people going to their doctors complaining of persistent pain may not have any apparent physical cause. Doctors can often be as mystified as their patients over what can be causing the pain. Even with improvements in diagnosis and treatment, chronic pain can have multiple causes that are often difficult to untangle. This can mean years of treatment as doctors experiment with different medications, therapies, and surgeries to try to alleviate the suffering.

So, is it any surprise that people with chronic pain are especially prone to depression? As we have already seen, depression often arises from a sense of helplessness that certain problems have no solution. People coping with long-term chronic pain often have to deal with additional problems such as loss of sleep, fatigue, worry about their financial future, and their long-term prospect for recovery. All of these factors are going to reduce their ability to cope with what they are experiencing. Add to that the sense that there is no apparent relief in sight, and feelings of depression are almost impossible to avoid.

Research looking at chronic pain patients suggests that guilt and uncertainty are two of the main factors that can contribute to depression. The guilt is often due to patients being unable to function as they once did due to the pain. This means being less able to care for themselves and having to depend on other people. Since chronic pain patients also have no idea how long their pain will continue, this sense of uncertainty can also lead them to feel helpless and despondent about the future.

But along with chronic pain causing depression, it is also possible for depressive symptoms to make the pain much worse. Depressed people are often going to ruminate about the problems in their life, and this frequent rumination will also make them less able to take their minds off the pain they are feeling. They are also prone to catastrophizing their pain (exaggerating symptoms to make them seem much worse than they actually are). As a result, their ability to cope with the pain is reduced as well.

Since chronic pain and depression often go together, therapists have developed specialized treatment programs to help patients learn to manage their pain and control depression as well. One program that has been particularly successful is cognitive behavioral therapy for chronic pain (CBT-CP). Developed by therapists at the Veterans Administration for treating injured veterans, CBT-CP teaches patients to manage their chronic pain as part of a comprehensive pain treatment program. They are taught valuable coping techniques including relaxation training, cognitive restructuring, and ways to prevent the kind of catastrophizing and rumination that make chronic pain worse. Numerous research studies have shown the benefits of joint chronic pain-depression treatment. It can also help prevent more severe problems from developing, including substance abuse and suicidal thinking.

While chronic pain can often be emotionally draining for many people, supportive counseling can be an effective way to learn better ways of coping. Check with your doctor if you are experiencing depression because of chronic pain.

24. Why is depression so common in the military?

As you are probably already aware, returning veterans, particularly veterans who have served highly dangerous tours of duty overseas are prone to a wide variety of mental health problems due to their experiences. In addition to posttraumatic stress disorder, returning veterans often face significant medical issues due to the injuries they've received.

This means treatment for chronic pain, traumatic brain injury, and other lengthy medical procedures. Not surprisingly, returning veterans, especially veterans who have been exposed to combat, are also prone to many of the behavioral problems linked to depression, including an increased risk of suicide, substance abuse, and self-injury.

Not that this is limited to veterans alone. Virtually anyone with posttraumatic symptoms resulting from exposure to combat stress is going to be more at risk for depression. Along with people serving in the military, these symptoms can appear in civilians as well. This includes refugees from war-torn countries, aid workers, journalists, and emergency responders. Studies looking at posttraumatic trauma following war typically find veterans reporting problems with depression, insomnia, irritability, concentration problems, and increased social isolation. These symptoms typically last much longer in veterans than in nonveterans as a rule, though there are prominent exceptions.

There also appear to be significant sex differences between male and female veterans in terms of reported problems with depression. This is often because men are less likely than women to admit to emotional problems unless the symptoms are severe enough to force them to seek help. Women veterans are also vulnerable to trauma that men may not typically experience, including sexual assault and sexual harassment. While men may also have such experiences, it is far less common than with women (men are also less likely to report such abuse). Though sexual abuse is becoming more widely recognized in the military, victims often feel isolated because of their experiences and the lack of support they receive.

When left untreated, the consequences of depression in current and former military personnel can be fatal. According to the most recent report released by the U.S. Department of Veterans Affairs, roughly twenty-two veterans die from suicide each day with an overall suicide rate twice that found in civilians. Though the overwhelming majority of these suicides are men, women veterans also have a suicide rate far higher than that found in civilians. Research has shown that posttraumatic stress, depression, hopelessness, and access to firearms significantly increase suicide risk in veterans. Traumatic brain injuries, even relatively mild injuries, can also increase suicide risk by making veterans less able to cope with the stress of returning to normal life and with managing their emotions.

Though most Veterans Administration hospitals have treatment programs in place to help veterans dealing with posttraumatic stress and depression, the waiting lists for these programs can mean months of delay before receiving treatment. Also, recent studies show that many veterans don't seek treatment until it is too late.

Despite the resistance many veterans may feel about asking for treatment, there are a wide range of options available in most communities. Veterans Administration therapists are even developing telehealth approaches for people in need who are living in remote communities or who may feel uncomfortable about seeing a counselor face-to-face. Check the appendix for contact information or for help finding the right program in your area.

25. Are sexual minorities more vulnerable to depression?

While different sexual minorities, including gays, lesbians, and transsexuals, have become more widely accepted in many places, they still face harassment and discrimination. Considering the stress of living in a society that regards heterosexual behavior as the norm, it's no wonder that most gays and lesbians prefer to keep their sexuality hidden if at all possible. And it's also no wonder that mental health problems such as depression can be so common as well.

For adolescents in particular, the kind of homophobic bullying faced by anyone who "seems" gay or lesbian can be devastating, especially for young people trying to come to terms with their own sense of identity. And many schools remain reluctant to do anything about it (though this is slowly changing). While some places have attempted to modernize sex education guidelines to help promote greater acceptance, this is often opposed by religious groups and parents, especially parents who come from cultures that are much more intolerant concerning same-sex relationships.

Along with greater vulnerability to depression, victims of this kind of bullying are prone to a wide variety of problems including substance abuse, academic problems, and even suicide. Cases involving children as young as nine who commit suicide due to homophobic bullying are hardly uncommon, though this rarely leads to significant improvement in how these children are treated.

Studies looking at lesbian, gay, bisexual, and transgender adolescents have found that as many as 31 percent have attempted suicide at least once and that depression and hopelessness can both play a role in suicide risk. The kind of emotional support received by sexual minority youths can also help protect them against depression and suicide. This includes the importance of having a strong emotional support network in place, whether that support comes from parents, siblings, friends, or concerned teachers or counselors. It is the sense of isolation that many sexual minority youths often feel that can be particularly damaging to their self-esteem and ability to cope.

In recent years, a number of new resources have become available for sexual minority youths dealing with depression or other emotional problems. As one example, the "It Gets Better" project was launched in 2010 by activist Dan Savage and his husband as a way of helping teens deal with homophobic bullying or who are considering suicide. Operating from its own website, the project features thousands of contributions from people sharing their own stories of bullying and abuse as well as how their lives have improved since high school.

For sexual minority youth or older adults dealing with depression, there are treatment resources available in most communities. Finding these resources may be difficult for many people reluctant to be open about their sexuality however. The appendix contains some suggestions of online resources that might be helpful in getting a referral to someone in your area.

Consequences of Depression

26. Can depression lead to drug or alcohol abuse?

Though not everyone dealing with depression will develop a drug or alcohol problem, there is no question that they often go together. According to the *National Epidemiologic Survey on Alcoholism and Related Conditions*, around 40 percent of people with a lifetime history of major depressive disorder (MDD) will develop a problem with alcohol. While the risk of depressed people becoming dependent on illegal drugs is much lower (17 percent), this is still far greater than we might expect from chance alone. For that matter, 30 percent of people with MDD will also become dependent on nicotine.

But why are depression and addiction found together so frequently? Intriguingly enough, some studies suggest that one possible reason for depression being much more common in women than in men is that men are more likely to rely on drugs or alcohol to control their symptoms. In one study looking at over twelve thousand Amish people (who have a cultural ban against drugs and alcohol), men and women were found to develop MDD at the same rate. This strongly suggests that undiagnosed depression may play an important role in substance abuse, at least in men.

Another possible explanation for this apparent link between substance abuse and depression deals with the effect that substance abuse has on the brain itself. For example, most addictive drugs work by producing a dopamine rush in key areas of the brain, including the ventral tegmental area of the midbrain. This leads to a sensation of pleasure and a strong need to seek out more of the drug to continue experiencing this pleasure. As the body adapts to continued use of the drug, users develop a physical dependence (i.e., their systems become dependent on regular dosages to avoid withdrawal symptoms) as well as a psychological dependence in which they come to rely on the drug to help cope with negative symptoms such as stress and depression.

For people who develop depression, drugs and alcohol can seem like an effective way of coping since it allows them to escape their symptoms, at least temporarily. Essentially, they have learned to medicate themselves through the use of various mind-altering substances, even if they are simply exchanging one problem for another.

Self-medication doesn't apply to depression alone, however. There are a wide variety of physical and psychological conditions that can lead people to experiment with different substances as a way of getting their problems under control. Self-medicators often experiment with different substances, including herbal remedies, over-the-counter medications bought at pharmacies, or drugs purchased illegally until they find something that seems to work. They can often justify self-medicating as a way of escaping from conventional medicine and taking personal control of their health.

Unfortunately, many of the substances they may decide to use are also addictive in their own right, and as a result, users may develop long-term substance abuse problems in addition to their original symptoms. For this reason, self-medication often ends up making their symptoms even worse and leads to even more serious medical problems.

There is considerable overlap between the symptoms of drug withdrawal and the symptoms of depression. For people who are going through withdrawal, depression is often reported during the early stages as their brain's biochemistry slowly returns to normal. How long this period of depression lasts often depends on what kind of addictive substance they are dealing with and how far back their addiction goes. For example, studies of patients who are withdrawing from alcohol suggests that depression is highest in the first week and drops slowly afterward.

Also, as we have seen, many users get started on drugs or alcohol because it was the only way to handle the depression they were feeling originally. This means that the depression will often persist even after they have successfully gotten "clean" of their addiction, something that may encourage them to start the entire drug/alcohol abuse cycle all over again.

Since the relationship between depression and substance abuse can often be very complicated, it is essential that people dealing with both depression and substance abuse seek medical help as soon as possible. Only a qualified health professional can make a proper diagnosis, especially for those patients dealing with more than one diagnosis. It also demonstrates how dangerous self-medication can be as a way of coping with depression.

We will be looking at different treatment options in later sections as well as exploring the kind of treatment that might be best for people dealing with other mental health problems in addition to depression.

27. Why are depression and anxiety often seen together?

Though people dealing with depression often develop other mental health issues such as substance abuse, fatigue, and insomnia, they appear especially prone to chronic anxiety. Research studies looking at patients with MDD have found that anywhere from 42 to 72 percent also report anxiety symptoms that are often just as distressing as depression.

According to the DSM-V, there are different types of anxiety disorders that can often co-occur with depression. These include:

- Generalized anxiety disorder (GAD). While we all experience day-to-day worries about different problems in our lives, people with GAD are prone to episodes of extreme worry, often without any apparent cause. The persistent anxiety seen in GAD can often be so severe that it becomes almost impossible to hold down a normal life. They are also much more easily startled, have trouble sleeping, and have various physical symptoms including headaches, sweating, and hot flashes.
- Panic disorder. People are prone to severe panic attacks, often without warning. Panic attack symptoms can include shortness of breath, shaking, tremors, and a sense that something terrible is about to happen. While episodes can often be controlled with medication, many people who experience panic attacks may find themselves afraid to leave their homes or do regular activities out of fear of having an attack in an unfamiliar setting.
- Posttraumatic stress disorder (PTSD). Already discussed elsewhere in this book, PTSD usually results from exposure to severely traumatic events and can result in emotional distress and flashbacks triggered by sensory stimuli that act as reminders of the trauma.

- More specific forms of anxiety disorders including separation anxiety (inability to handle being separated from one's home or attachment figures), different phobias (irrational fear of specific objects or themes), and health anxiety disorder (also known as hypochondria, or the fear of illness).

Though the symptoms for these different disorders can be very different, they are all characterized by overwhelming worry that can often strike in a wide variety of ways. As you might expect, such symptoms can be especially devastating for people already dealing with depression (and vice versa).

In many cases, experiencing chronic anxiety can often cause depression to develop due to the despair people feel over symptoms of anxiety that don't seem to go away. Chronic depression can often produce chronic anxiety as well due to persistent fears about the future and whether the depression will ever improve.

Whatever the causes or whether the anxiety or the depression begins first, people experiencing both types of symptoms are often much harder to treat than patients developing one disorder alone. While there are different medications that can be used to treat chronic depression and different kinds of anxiety disorders, there is no one medication that can be used to treat both at once. People dealing with both depression and anxiety may often need to try different medications as well as different treatment programs to help them come to terms with their symptoms.

For both chronic anxiety and depression, the key to getting the right kind of help is to be open about your symptoms and to ask for help. These symptoms never go away on their own.

28. How does depression affect families?

The important thing to remember about depression is that it never just affects the person who has it but also the people around them. This includes family members, friends, coworkers, fellow students, or just about anyone that a depressed person interacts with on a regular basis.

Someone dealing with depression is going to be prone to feelings of self-doubt, isolation, and the sense of being worthless and unloved. This is where the emotional support that friends and family can provide can be critical in keeping the depression from getting worse. Though they may not have experienced depression themselves and often have misconceptions about what is happening to a loved one with these symptoms, their very willingness to be there for that person and refusal to give up on them can help with the process of recovery.

Research studies looking at the impact of family support on depression show that supportive family members can help buffer the stresses of life that can often lead to depression. Even though family members can find this frustrating due to feelings of helplessness, simply reminding the person affected that depression is treatable and that they will get better in time may be enough.

But the burden of dealing with a depressed family member is frequently draining, especially for someone with a depressed spouse or a parent with a depressed child. Acting as a full-time caregiver for someone with depression is an enormous challenge. Even when the depression is relatively mild, encouraging depressed people to be more active, to take proper care of themselves, or even to communicate more can be a thankless task. Many depressed people may even resent these efforts or view themselves as being hopeless.

Along with caretaking responsibilities, caregivers may also be required to do many of those activities that depressed people may not have the energy to do themselves. This can include managing finances, taking over work responsibilities (if possible), and interacting with legal and government services on their behalf.

Considering the kind of strain faced by caregivers, it's hardly surprising that they are especially prone to developing emotional problems themselves, not to mention the physical problems that go along with chronic stress. While friends and family members may try to take over some of this burden, it is extremely easy to burn out because of the pressures as well as develop a sense of hopelessness if the depression fails to improve.

For family members dealing with a depressed person, it is vital that they learn to take care of themselves as well as their loved one. This means making time for themselves by getting out socially and doing the kind of things they enjoy. But they also need to be more open about the frustration that often results from providing this kind of care. Caregivers need to take care of their personal health by making sure to eat and exercise properly and finding outlets for the frequent stress that caregiving can bring.

Though caregivers often end up feeling completely alone, there are resources available in the community that can help, including support groups for people dealing with this kind of stress. Check with local or online mental health care resources for contact numbers.

29. What are the real costs of depression to society?

As we have seen in Question 3, over 10 to 16 million adult Americans and over 3.1 million U.S. adolescents will develop symptoms of depression severe enough to be considered a serious impairment. And these figures don't take into account those people who are never diagnosed, who are diagnosed with other health problems, or who commit suicide.

The World Health Organization estimates that there are over three hundred million people with severe depression worldwide making it the fourth leading cause of disability overall (and will have risen to the number-two spot by 2020). Though numerous research studies have been carried out to estimate the actual impact of depression to society, this can be extremely difficult considering that many people suffering from severe depression are never diagnosed or receive treatment.

According to one recent U.S. study published in 2015, the total economic burden of MDD alone is approximately $210.5 billion a year (up from $173.2 billion a year in 2005). Along with the actual costs of treatment, this figure also includes the economic costs of time lost from work, reduced productivity, and shortened work careers caused by long-term disability and suicide. According to the report's authors, depression "is the leading cause of disability for people aged 15–44, resulting in almost 400 million disability days per year, substantially more than more other physical and mental conditions."

But there are other costs that are harder to determine. As we have already seen, many people who suffer from symptoms of depression may turn to drugs or alcohol to medicate themselves. Considering that substance abuse is a major health problem in its own right, this means that the effects of depression may be more far-reaching than anyone realizes. For that matter, depression can be linked to other health problems including chronic pain, insomnia, anxiety, adjustment problems, and posttraumatic disorders.

Also, as we have seen in Question 27, many of the economic and health problems linked to depression can also affect family members who need to dedicate themselves to caring for affected loved ones. This can mean lost time from work and reduced productivity due to time lost from work as well as stress-related medical issues. The long-term costs may be even greater considering that caregivers may often be in need of health services themselves due to the impact of chronic stress.

Though the actual costs associated with depression may be impossible to estimate, it's clear to see that it represents a major drain on health resources around the world. While research has shown that providing better treatment for people with depression can help reduce some of these costs, as well as make life better overall, making these treatment options available worldwide continues to be an enormous challenge.

30. Are people with depression at risk for suicide?

Numerous research studies have consistently shown that well over 90 percent of all people who committed suicide or attempted it were suffering from some form of mental illness (usually untreated). The single most common diagnosis linked to suicide is major depression (occurring in 56 to 87 percent of cases), closely followed by substance abuse (26 to 55 percent), and schizophrenia (6 to 13 percent). Though diagnoses such as anxiety disorder are also common, they are usually seen in conjunction with depression.

Considering that people who commit suicide often don't leave notes or provide reasons for their actions, most of the research linking suicide to depression and other mental health problems comes from studying suicide *attempts*. Though these attempts are much more common than actual suicide, studies show that more than one-third of those who succeed at committing suicide have made at least one previous attempt at it. This is why doctors often ask patients with depression about suicidal thoughts and why having attempted suicide at least once is a strong risk factor for future attempts.

In looking specifically at how depression and suicide are related, a 1997 study of more than eleven thousand patients showed that being diagnosed with unipolar depression significantly increases the risk of suicide. Bipolar disorder may also increase the risk of suicide depending on how severe the symptoms are.

Despite these findings, it is still important to recognize that most people dealing with depression are not going to kill themselves (and at least half never even try). But there are risk factors that can make depressed people particularly vulnerable to suicidal thoughts and actions. For example, the greatest risk of suicide occurring in people with depression is during those first few months as they are still learning to deal with their symptoms. For someone who had never had a depressive episode before, experiencing those kinds of symptoms, along with feelings of hopelessness, guilt, reduced appetite, and insomnia can be devastating.

Research looking at first-time depression patients found that suicide risk rises sharply soon after being admitted to hospital and also after being discharged. This is why patients need to be carefully monitored during the early days of admission and after they are released into the community, especially if they don't have family members or friends to take care of them.

Dealing with other mental health issues aside from depression can also increase suicide risk. This can include drug or alcohol problems, anxiety disorders, long-term personality issues, or serious medical illnesses. Also, as we have seen, having made a previous suicide attempt is the biggest risk factor, especially if it is a recent attempt.

Under certain circumstances, even being on medication to control depression or bipolar disorder can increase suicide risk in some patients. For people dealing with multiple symptoms such as anxiety, the antidepressant may only curb the depression and cause the other symptoms to feel much more severe as a result. This is why patients being placed on medication for the first time need to be carefully questioned about suicidal history as well as be warned about the potential side effects of their medication.

As we can see, the risk of suicide in people with depression cannot be overlooked. Sadly, the greatest risk is going to be in the ones who are afraid to ask for help and who hide their symptoms from friends and family members. If you or someone you know is feeling suicidal, just recognize that there are resources out there that can help. Even if you are afraid to talk to a doctor face-to-face, online resources and nationwide hotlines are also available. Check the appendix for some recommendations.

Culture, Media, and Depression

31. How do different cultures view depression?

This can be a difficult question to answer considering that international surveys looking at depression across different countries show dramatic differences in terms of who is likely to develop symptoms. For that matter, there are some languages that don't even have a *word* for what we would call depression.

Also, considering the stigma surrounding mental illnesses in different cultures, the number of people seeking help for their symptoms is going to vary widely from one country to the next. For people living in Japan, for example, only about 3 percent of the population will seek help for depression while countries such as the United States have a substantially higher percentage of people asking for help. But, does this mean that people in other cultures are less likely to develop depression? Or are they just less likely to *admit* being depressed?

Cross-cultural studies of depression conducted since the 1980s strongly suggest that culture differences can have a dramatic impact on the type of depressive symptoms people can show, how likely they are to be diagnosed at all, and how likely they are to seek out some kind of help. Considering the deep stigma against mental illness found in many places, it isn't surprising that most people feeling depressed would prefer to keep it hidden, often until it's too late.

In fact, some psychiatrists have argued that depression as we know it is mainly a Western disease that is nonexistent in some societies. For example, when psychiatrist Emil Kraepelin visited Indonesia in the early years of the twentieth century, he concluded that depression was almost nonexistent. A similar conclusion was made by psychiatrist John Colin Carothers when he wrote about depression in Africans. As far as he was concerned, any mental health issues that developed were due to their exposure to Western culture and values as well as the effects of colonization.

Even into the late 1980s, medical anthropologists continued to challenge the idea of depression in non-Western cultures though this is not a popular viewpoint today. Part of the problem is that the way people express emotional distress, including symptoms of depression, varies widely depending on their cultural background and beliefs about mental illness.

For that matter, people in other cultures may also report problems that resemble what we call depression but which do not appear to have any real comparison in Western countries (except among immigrants). As we have already seen in Question 9, these conditions can go by different names, including *pena* and *susto* in parts of Latin America, *brain fag* in West Africa, *dhat* on the Indian subcontinent, *tawatl ye sni* (totally discouraged) among the Dakota Sioux, *shenjing shairuo* in Chinese culture, and so on.

While the diagnosis may vary depending on where we happen to be living in the world, the actual symptoms are usually not that different. Whether or not people dealing with depression actually get help is often going to depend on the kind of mental health services that are available. Unfortunately, this is a particular problem in poorer countries that have only a few psychiatrists or other mental health professionals. This often means critical delays in treatment as a result. While international health agencies such as the World Health Organization are trying to increase awareness about disorders such as depression, much more needs to be done.

32. How are goth and emo subcultures linked to depression?

Beginning in the early 1980s in England, the goth subculture rapidly spread to North America where it became an extremely popular alternative to more dominant music cultures. Inspired by the "gothic rock" of bands such as The Doors as well as gothic horror movies, art, and literature, "goths" (as fans were often called) could usually be identified by their preference for "edgy" bands such as Bauhaus, Sisters of Mercy, and The Cure. Along with a conspicuously gloomy attitude, black hair, black eyeliner, dark fingernail polish, goths also preferred to wear "somber" clothing copied from the styles of previous centuries as well as to imitate the "cultured decadence" found in classic horror novels as written by Anne Rice and other authors.

While not as popular as it once was, the goth movement continues to attract followers worldwide and has become linked to other subculture movements such as punk rock and death music. Another popular subculture often identified with goth is the emo subculture. Though the actual origin of the word *emo* is obscure, this music genre is usually identified by the emotional expression, hardcore (and often confessional) lyrics, and the distinctive fashion styles preferred by fans.

Similar to goth styles in many ways, emo fans have a preference for studded belts, black wristbands, flat hair, and long bangs that often cover the face. In the same way that goth fans are called goths, emo fans tend to be referred to as emo kids or, simply, emos.

For both goths and emos, however, media stories have long suggested that some marginalized youths belonging to these subcultures have been involved in rampage shootings. The most well-known example was the 1999 Columbine Massacre in which the two youths responsible were described in news stories as being part of a goth "cult." Later research has disputed this conclusion and suggests that goths and emos are far more likely to be *victims* of violence rather than engaging in violence themselves. Still, the stigma surrounding goth and emo youths often leads to their being viewed with suspicion by police, teachers, and parents' groups.

But there is far more evidence showing that youths who identify themselves as goth or emo are prone to self-harm behavior and suicide attempts. For example, a 2006 study examining more than twelve hundred youths from ages eleven to nineteen showed that lifetime rates of self-harm and suicide attempts was highest among youths who identified themselves as strong goths. Even adjusting for other factors such as substance use and history of depression did little to change the results.

A later study published in 2015 showed that youths who self-identified as goths at the age of fifteen were up to three times more likely to be diagnosed with depression at the age of eighteen than non-goths. Similar results were also found for the likelihood of self-harm attempts even when other possible contributing factors were taken into account. While there is relatively little research looking at youths who are part of the emo subculture, available results suggest that emo youths may also be at an increased risk for depression and self-harm.

Though there is evidence of a link between goth/emo membership and depression, it still isn't clear why this relationship exists. Does being part of the goth or emo scene cause suicidal depression or are people who are already prone to these mental health issues more likely to become goths or emo kids? In fact, researchers have suggested that young people who are already feeling suicidal may actually *benefit* from joining goth or emo groups. Not only does being part of a larger movement provide young people with a sense of belonging but the friends they make in these communities can also provide them with emotional support.

As we can see, simply being a part of the goth or emo scenes don't necessarily mean that young people will attempt suicide. Still, family members need to be alert to the different signs of depression that we have already discussed in previous sections. If you are worried about a friend or family member, it is important to let health professionals know as soon as possible.

33. Can social media make depression worse?

For most young people, spending time online on many of the different social media platforms out there has become an essential part of staying in contact with friends and acquaintances from around the world. Along with Facebook and Twitter, they can also rely on Instagram, Facebook Messenger, YouTube, Reddit, and Pinterest, to name just a few.

Not surprisingly, researchers have been taking a closer look at these different platforms and what their regular use can have on the emotions of people using them. What they have found suggests that, while social media can allow people to socialize with friends and family without ever leaving their homes, it can also make users feel more isolated than ever.

Facebook, for example, has become a way of life for hundreds of millions of people who log on each day. Along with the free exchange of news, selfies, and whatever viral memes happen to be popular at the given moment, Facebook also allows for regular interactions among people who may never even meet in real life but who can still be considered friends.

Considering the power that Facebook and other platforms seem to have, it's probably not surprising that more and more anecdotes are emerging about the dark side of this kind of social contact. Stories of cyberbullying, mean-spirited comments, cyberstalking, and misunderstandings seem rampant, especially for young females dealing with unwanted attention. Despite efforts to curb the worst examples of this kind of abuse, the negative experiences, as described by many people, can have a powerful impact in terms of low self-esteem, depression, and social anxiety. It's probably also not surprising that new research is highlighting the effect that negative experiences on Facebook and other social media platforms can have on depression.

One study published in 2013 looked at 264 young adults who were recruited to determine how the introduction of Facebook may have affected their emotional well-being, Along with examining the frequency, severity, and nature of the negative comments the research participants reported over time, they also completed measures of different depressive symptoms. What the researchers found was that 82 percent of all participants reported at least one negative Facebook experience overall and 55 percent reported one in the year before they took part in the study. About 63 percent said they had four or more such negative experiences. When compared to the 24 percent of participants reporting moderate-to-severe depression, overall risk of depression was 3.2 times greater in participants reporting negative experiences than those who had not. These results were particularly impressive, as it took other factors such as childhood mental health problems into account as well.

As you might expect, people reporting mean or bullying Facebook posts were 3.5 times more likely to develop depression while people receiving unwanted contacts (such as cyberstalking) were 2.5 times more likely to do so. How frequently these experiences occurred also made a difference. People reporting receiving four or more of these posts had a substantially higher risk of depression than people who didn't.

While more research is needed, these results highlight the emotional impact these negative posts can have. All online users, but especially adolescents and young adults, need to be aware of the emotional risks associated with social media platforms, particularly Facebook. Though many people may rely on the Internet as a personal lifeline for staying in touch with others, learning to balance that with in-person social contacts can help prevent the "Facebook blues" that seem to have become so common in recent years.

34. Why is there such stigma surrounding depression?

For centuries, people suffering from different kinds of mental illness have often been treated as outcasts. Not only were they often regarded as being possessed by demons (and still are in some parts of the world), people regarded as "odd" or "sick" were often either forced into hospitals where they would live the rest of their lives or else kept hidden by family members who feared for their reputation. As recently as a generation ago, mental illness was something that people refused to talk about, even when it applied to a close family member.

Even today, people still use words like *crazy*, *wacko*, *nuts*, *psycho*, *loco*, and *mental case* to describe people or ideas that are out of the ordinary. Certainly, there are no end of television shows and horror movies depicting people with mental illness as unpredictable or dangerous. Not only are these attitudes found in just about every society but are often seen in young children who have no difficulty in using labels like *weird* or *coo-coo* with other children they see as different from themselves.

Despite attempts at changing these attitudes about mental illness, the stigma that often surrounds people dealing with psychiatric issues remains strong. Even in Western countries where psychiatric treatment is widely available, many people suffering from serious mental disorders such as schizophrenia may end up becoming homeless since they have nowhere else to live. For that matter, jails and prisons have become the largest mental health facilities in the United States and in many other countries.

While attitudes and misconceptions about depression always have the potential to be hurtful, there are two potential scenarios that can be especially dangerous. The first of these scenarios occurs when this kind of stigma affects how people with depression see themselves. People who consider themselves to be "crazy" or "hopeless" may give in to despair or refuse to seek help. The second scenario is when friends or family members either refuse to take depression seriously or else treat it as something "shameful" that needs to be kept hidden (a common attitude in many cultures).

People with depression need to be realistic about their symptoms and also need the emotional support of other people in their lives so that they can properly heal. As we can see, the stigma surrounding depression and other treatable conditions can often make people hesitant in asking for help. It is this need to "stay in the closet" that can lead people suffering from depression to hide what is happening for as long as they can. This also means delaying treatment for much longer than necessary, which can lead to the symptoms becoming even worse with time.

Though changing public attitudes about conditions such as depression won't be easy, progress is still being made. In recent years, many well-known people and their family members have come forward to talk about their symptoms as a way of decreasing the stigma associated with depression. Kristen Bell, Johnny Depp, Harrison Ford, Gwyneth Paltrow, Lady Gaga, Dolly Parton, and J. K. Rowling are just a few of the names of people who have tried to put a human face on depression and make it easier for others to come forward as well.

So don't be afraid to be as open as possible about depression, whether you are dealing with it yourself or helping a friend or close family member. Fighting the stigma surrounding mental illness can be one of the most important ways of helping people with depression move on with their lives.

Treatment, Prevention, and Life after Depression

35. How can people with depression find help?

While someone dealing with depression may feel isolated and alone, getting help is probably easier now than it ever has been in the past. Not only are most family doctors, nurses, social workers, and other health care professionals getting better training for helping patients who are depressed but community mental health programs offering treatment for depression can be found in most urban areas. Even for people living in rural areas without easy access to treatment centers, there are also national hotlines that can be called toll-free from just about anywhere in the country. And then there are the online resources that provide information about depression as well as free consultation and listings for local agencies that can help.

As we've already seen in previous questions, the first step for someone seeking help for symptoms of depression typically involves seeing a family doctor first and having a complete checkup. Since a family doctor already has a complete medical history, he or she can quickly rule out other possible explanations for the symptoms. A family doctor can also prescribe medication that might help as well. It is still important to get all the necessary information first, including possible side effects or drug interaction effects, before agreeing to take that medication however.

Even for those people who decide against medication, there are a wide range of alternative treatments, and their doctor is likely the best referral source for mental health services in their area. This can include individual psychotherapists, mental health clinics, or the local hospital depending on how severe the symptoms are and what treatment options happen to be available nearby.

Unfortunately, many of these services tend to be concentrated in the larger cities, and people living in rural areas may have trouble finding the help they need. Many people dealing with depression, especially adolescents and teenagers, might also be reluctant to talk to a counselor face-to-face.

One alternative that is becoming increasingly popular for many people with depression is accessing mental health care online or using one of the toll-free hotlines maintained by many national organizations (some examples are provided in the appendix). Most of these hotlines are serviced at all times by trained counselors or volunteers who can offer support as well as provide information about local resources that might be available. For many people with depression, much of the appeal for these services stems from the ability to access them anonymously. For adolescents and teens feeling suicidal or dealing with issues that they may be reluctant to share with their parents, online sites or hotlines can literally be a lifesaver in many cases.

Along with sites for national organizations, there are also chat room sites where people can discuss specific issues and interact with others who might be going through the same issues themselves. Some of these chat sites are part of a large community with users from across the country who have a variety of interests and personal issues that they might want to talk about. Make sure that the chat site you are using is being moderated to avoid dealing with "trolls" who may sabotage the conversation with malicious posts.

No matter the advice that you may receive, whether online or in person, it is always up to you to make the final decision about the kind of treatment you want. It's also important to recognize that there is no miracle cure or "quick fix" when dealing with depression. This is why it is important never to give up hope and, if the first attempt at seeking help doesn't work out, to not be afraid to try again.

36. What are some of the most common forms of treatment for children and adults dealing with depression?

There are a wide range of different treatment options available for helping children, adolescents, and adults dealing with depression. Still, there is no one-size-fits-all approach, and the treatment that people with depression may receive will often depend on what symptoms they happen to be showing, their life history, the treatment they have received in the past, and the progress they are making over time.

For most people seeking help for depression, whether they are adolescents or adults, treatment usually begins with an evaluation to determine how to proceed and also to start developing a treatment plan (see Question 37). This is basically a road map that will help guide people through the treatment process. Also, depending on how severe the symptoms are and whether there are additional problems such as substance abuse, suicidal thoughts, or anxiety, some people may require round-the-clock care in an inpatient facility.

In most cases, however, depression can usually be treated with a combination of antidepressant medication and psychotherapy. Though the medication may be prescribed by either a family physician or a psychiatrist, psychotherapy usually begins with one-to-one sessions with a trained psychologist or counselor. The main purpose of individual treatment is to make clients comfortable enough to be willing to open up about their depression and other related issues. It is also through individual sessions that clients can start talking about other issues that may be triggering their mood problems. This can include having a history of childhood physical or sexual abuse, posttraumatic symptoms, family concerns, social anxiety, and so on. Many clients may prefer to deal exclusively with individual counseling while others may prefer to move into group treatment as soon as possible.

One of the advantages of individual counseling is the added privacy that it provides. This means that clients can open up in a way they might not feel comfortable doing in a group setting. Individual counseling can either be open ended or with a fixed number of sessions. Open-ended treatment means that sessions will continue until such time that the client is seen as ready to try group treatment. In addition to individual counseling, people in therapy may also be seen in family counseling sessions with participating family members to learn how to work together to overcome the depression.

For many patients who have successfully completed individual counseling and who feel ready to talk about their emotional problems more openly, the next step is to join a therapy group. The type of therapy offered often depends on what the person in treatment hopes to achieve. Groups can include:

• Psychoeducation training programs. Much as the name suggests, these programs focus on educating depressed patients about their emotional issues and the barriers they may face in learning to move on with their lives. Training modules can include anger management, relaxation training, good nutrition and exercise, and meditation.

- Skill development programs. Using an interactive training approach allowing group members to share their own insights and ideas, these group sessions focus on training members to handle anger effectively, forming stronger social networks, coping strategies, relaxation training, and recognizing the triggers that can lead to negative thinking.

- Cognitive behavioral psychotherapy (CBT). In a CBT group, members are trained in how to recognize and change maladaptive beliefs and behaviors that can reinforce negative thoughts and beliefs. One of the central principles of CBT is to learn how to anticipate problems and develop self-control using effective coping strategies. Cognitive behavioral strategies can include cognitive restructuring, problem solving, stress inoculation training, relaxation training, mindfulness, and relapse prevention techniques (see Question 42 for more information).

While most patients can receive treatment on a weekly basis, people with long-standing depression and a history of relapses may require much more intensive treatment than what is usually offered. They may also need more intensive monitoring of the medications they are receiving including whether they are experiencing side effects that are complicating their recovery.

Even after treatment is completed, therapists and their patients need to decide on what will happen next. Many users who have completed treatment may choose to attend maintenance treatment sessions with their counselor on a monthly or bimonthly basis. This allows the counselor to monitor the progress being made as well as give patients the chance to review material covered during the treatment sessions and share details of new concerns as they arise. It is also important for patients who have completed treatment to remember that the risk of relapsing into depression may always be present and avoid the kind of triggers that could lead to a setback. Many of the different treatment options available to people with depression will be covered in more detail in the next few sections.

37. What is a treatment plan?

As we have already seen, there is no such thing as a one-size-fits-all treatment for depression. The kind of treatment needed will vary widely depending on the age of the person requesting help, whether there are related mental health problems that also need to be treated, whether the patient is suffering from medical problems that can complicate recovery, and whether the treatment professional needs to deal with other issues such as childhood abuse or trauma.

For anyone seeking treatment, the first step begins with meeting with a counselor and formulating a treatment plan that outlines the goals that need to be met and the type of treatment that might be needed to achieve those goals. Once the goals are laid out, the therapist and the client then establish priorities (i.e., which goals need to be met first and which can be addressed later). While the primary goal of treatment will be to learn how to cope with depression, there are also going to be secondary goals that can include improving family relationships, learning to be more social, repairing problems at work or school that may have originated because of emotional issues, and so on. As part of the treatment plan, the therapist and the client also need to work out which goals can be achieved in the short term (i.e., within the next six months) and which are more long term. Achieving the short-term goals can often provide treatment clients with the confidence they need to stay in treatment.

The important thing to remember is that no two treatment plans are the same. Even if two people with similar problems enter treatment at the same time, the goals they will set are often very different. The treatment each will need is going to be shaped by their different life experiences and the different problems they will be trying to overcome as well as their individual strengths and weaknesses.

With many treatment plans, the first step involves developing a problem list. As you might expect, this means itemizing those problems that the patient happens to be experiencing *at that point in time.* Over the course of treatment, the problem list is going to change, as old problems become more manageable and new problems crop up. In developing the problem list, the patient needs to be able to describe the problem clearly and also come up with concrete ways of measuring the progress they will make in dealing with that problem.

For example, the problem could be stated as "I can't be around other people." The concrete evidence for this problem could include complaints from friends or family members over ducking social responsibilities. Additional evidence for this problem could include hiding in your room, skipping school or work, and so on. Other problems that can go on the problem list include emotional issues such as social anxiety or substance abuse.

The next step is to outline the short-term and long-term goals that patients would like to accomplish. While overcoming depression can be considered a long-term goal, patients and their therapists also need to identify more short-term goals that could act as signposts that indicate the progress being made. Achieving these goals can help patients gain the confidence they need to continue in treatment and learn how to get their lives back on track.

Once the goals are established, the next step is to outline the type of treatment to be used to help patients achieve the goals. Over the course of the treatment period, the treatment plan is periodically reviewed to determine how successful the patient has been at meeting the original goals.

As these goals are met, the treatment plan often changes as well depending on what is happening in the patient's life and the progress that ends up being made. Since relapses are often going to happen, patients are encouraged to treat these episodes as learning opportunities and form new goals that can help them regain their confidence and avoid relapses in the future.

Even after the treatment ends and the patient manages to meet all the planned goals, the treatment plan can continue to act as a road map for future progress by outlining the different ways that patients can maintain the progress they have made. This can include maintenance sessions once every six months so patients can review what they have learned and establishing additional long-term goals that patients can continue to try achieving over time.

38. How do antidepressant medications work?

In a real sense, the use of chemical compounds to treat the symptoms of depression is as old as medicine itself. Traditional healers have long depended on such herbal compounds as St. John's Wort, *xiao yao*, "holy basil," poppy extract, cannabis, and so on for treating depression or melancholia (as it was commonly known).

While the actual benefit of these various herbal remedies remains controversial, one of the first modern antidepressants, reserpine, was first developed in the 1950s from another traditional remedy, a tea made from the *Rauwolfia* plant found in many parts of Asia and Africa. Long used as a treatment for insanity, fever, and snakebite, Western scientists took a closer look at *Rauwolfia* and learned to synthesize it under laboratory conditions. Despite early success in treating depressed patients using reserpine, problems with side effects spurred researchers to search for better alternatives.

Over the past six decades, medical researchers have developed a wide range of different medications for the treatment of conditions such as depression. While a full description of these different drugs would run into thousands of pages, they usually fall into three specific categories:

- Tricyclic antidepressants. Among the earliest antidepressant medications to be developed, tricyclic antidepressants (TCAs for short) have largely been replaced by more modern medications due to their frequent side effects, though they can still be used to treat depression symptoms in acute cases. Including such drugs as imipramine, amitriptyline, desipramine, and nortriptyline, TCAs work by directly acting on neurotransmitters such as serotonin and norepinephrine to increase their levels in the brain. Unfortunately, TCAs are also well known for side effects such as dry mouth; constipation; blurred vision; and, in many cases, sexual problems, excessive sweating, tremors, and weight changes. More rarely, it can also lead to seizures, disorientation (especially in older adults), and changes in heart rate. There is also the risk of drug interactions, which can lead to excessively high serotonin levels in the brain resulting in a "serotonin syndrome" with symptoms such as rapid heart rate, agitation, lack of coordination, and excessive sweating.
- MAO inhibitors. First developed in the 1950s, monoamine oxidase inhibitors (MAOIs) act on the brain by inhibiting the monoamine oxidase enzyme, which breaks down serotonin, norepinephrine, and dopamine to make them inactive. By inhibiting this enzyme's activity, MAOIs allow these neurotransmitters to stay much longer in the brain than they normally would. Because they also affect dopamine levels in the brain, MAOIs can also be used to treat Parkinson's disease. Popular MAOIs include isocarboxazid, phenelzine, selegiline, and tranylcypromine. These drugs are also known to cause many of the same side effects seen in TCAs along with insomnia and headaches and can also lead to serotonin syndrome depending on drug interactions. People taking MAOIs also need to follow dietary restrictions and avoid foods high in tyramine, which can affect blood pressure, as well as avoid alcohol. Due to these potential complications, MAOIs are not commonly used today, as safer alternatives are now available.
- Selective serotonin reuptake inhibitors. More commonly referred to as SSRIs, these are the most commonly prescribed antidepressant medications used today. By selectively acting on serotonin receptor sites while only weakly affecting dopamine and norepinephrine receptors,

SSRIs can significantly boost serotonin levels in the brain. As a result, they can relieve the symptoms of severe depression with far fewer side effects than other kinds of medication. Along with depression, SSRIs have been used in treating other conditions such as anxiety and obsessive-compulsive disorders. Some of the most well-known SSRIs are citalopram, fluoxetine, escitalopram, sertraline, and vilazodone, though others have already been approved by government regulators for treating depression and other disorders. Side effects still occur, though they are usually temporary. They include drowsiness; blurred vision; headaches; insomnia; and diarrhea and, more rarely, serotonin syndrome, if used in combination with some other medications.

There are other types of antidepressant medications available including atypical antipsychotics (mostly used with bipolar disorder), norepinephrine-dopamine reuptake inhibitors, and serotonin-norepinephrine reuptake inhibitors, to name some of the most common alternatives. The kind of medication that someone with depression will receive often depends on the nature of the symptoms, whether there are other medical issues that might affect how the drug works, and the training that the prescribing doctor has received. As for the actual risks associated with these different medications, we will explore that further in the next section.

39. Are there risks associated with taking antidepressant medication?

Even if a doctor recommends starting on an antidepressant medication, the final decision about whether or not this is a good idea belongs to the person who is going to take them. Still, while medication can help many people with depression control their symptoms, it isn't necessarily the best solution for everyone. Before starting any medication, it is essential to do some basic research about that medication, including becoming fully aware of the potential side effects and other risks involved. Here are just a few caveats that need to be considered:

- First of all, it takes time for most medications to build up in the system before the benefits become noticeable. For many people, this can mean weeks before their symptoms start to subside.
- Medications don't work the same way for everybody who takes them. Though some people start recovering right away, many people with depression may require trying several different medications before

finding one that works. For people with more than one diagnosis—depression and social anxiety, for example—a combination of different medications may be needed to get all the different symptoms under control. This can increase the risk of drug interaction effects as well as side effects.

- All medication needs to be carefully monitored by the prescribing doctor, including regular blood tests and frequent checkups to ensure that the medication is working as prescribed.
- Most importantly, it is essential that people taking antidepressant medication be alert to the possibility of suicidal thinking. Research looking at the effects of SSRIs on depression suggests that people who are already experiencing suicidal thoughts may find this kind of thinking becomes worse while on the medication. This is especially true for children and adolescents on SSRIs who seem particularly vulnerable to increased suicidal thinking and suicide attempts (but not necessarily successful attempts). This is why doctors need to be careful in screening their patients for suicidal thinking or previous attempts *before* prescribing antidepressant medication. If you or someone you know starts experiencing suicidal thoughts more frequently after starting on a new medication, seek help immediately.
- Ironically, the greatest danger for suicide in people who are dealing with depression isn't when the symptoms are at their worst, but when they are starting to feel better. Though this sounds like a contradiction, it really isn't. People dealing with severe depression are usually too despondent and immobilized to make any suicide plans. But when those symptoms ease, whether due to medication or some other treatment, many people may consider suicide out of fear that their condition will eventually get worse. This is another reason why doctors need to screen patients for suicidal thoughts before and after prescribing a new medication.
- There is also some controversy whether certain kinds of antidepressant medication may actually *cause* suicidal thinking, especially in people who are taking these medications for reasons other than treating depression (such as social anxiety). While this controversy is far from settled, people considering going on medication need to stay alert to new mental health issues that may arise.

Though newer medications have fewer potential problems, it is still essential that people who have been prescribed an unfamiliar medication do their research and make certain they are aware of all the potential risks. Though the doctor prescribing the medication will be monitoring your condition as well, the symptoms you are experiencing are an important clue to determine how well this medication is working.

Again, though, medication isn't necessarily the answer for everyone dealing with depression. We will explore a few alternatives in the next section.

40. What are some of the alternatives to drug treatment?

In addition to psychotherapy and treatment with antidepressant medication, there are some alternatives available.

Among the most well known are as follows:

Electroconvulsive therapy. One of the controversial alternative treatments for depression is electroconvulsive therapy (ECT), which was first developed in the 1930s. Basically involving the running of small electric currents through the brain, ECT is frequently effective in treating people with severe depression who don't respond to other forms of treatment. It is still unclear why this treatment works, though research studies have demonstrated its effectiveness in 50 to 70 percent of the cases. While modern ECT is typically conducted under a general anesthetic to avoid trauma, the notoriety resulting from its misuse during the 1940s and 1950s has given ECT a stigma that makes many patients extremely reluctant to try it even if recommended by a doctor. Anyone considering trying ECT needs to be aware of potential side effects including some memory loss, temporary mental confusion, nausea, and other medical complications depending on the patient's medical history.

Transcranial electrical stimulation. A more modern variation on ECT, transcranial electrical stimulation (tES) involves the running of minimal electric currents through scalp electrodes applied to different points along the skull. Depending on the polarity of the current, electrical stimulation can either increase or decrease cortical activity in the regions where the current is applied. First used to treat depression in the 1960s, interest in tES declined for many years due to its association with ECT. Since the 1990s, however, numerous research studies have found tES to be as effective as different antidepressant medications with almost no side effects. Along with relieving depressive symptoms, tES has also been used to boost cognitive functioning, including improved memory, concentration, and problem-solving ability. Some studies have also found positive results in treating some kinds of dementia such as Alzheimer's disease (at least in the early stages). While tES is certainly promising, the negative stigma surrounding ECT still makes it controversial. Also, some companies are offering "do-it-yourself" tES kits to allow people to treat themselves at home despite medical warnings about the dangers involved. As with any other form of treatment for depression, do your research first, and make sure the treatment professional is properly qualified.

Transcranial magnetic stimulation. As an alternative to the use of direct electric currents, transcranial magnetic stimulation (TMS) involves the use of shifting magnetic fields to induce an electric flow in target regions of the brain. Most forms of TMS involve the use of a magnetic field generator, or "coil," that can be applied to the head of the patient receiving treatment using a specialized headband. These coils are available in different sizes and configurations to allow very precise placement. Also, depending on how the magnetic fields are applied, it is also possible to stimulate the deeper structures of the brain, which can't be reached with surface electrodes as with ECT or tES. Along with its value in treating depression, TMS has also been used in treating neuropathic pain and boosting cognitive functioning in dementia cases as well as in diagnosing different types of neurological damage. While most applications of TMS are experimental at this point, it has shown great promise as a therapeutic treatment with few, if any, side effects being found.

For most people suffering from depression, some combination of psychotherapy and antidepressant medication will probably be all that they may need to help with their symptoms. Still, as newer treatment methods such as TMS and tES become more widely accepted, people needing help will likely benefit from having more options available to them.

41. Do herbal and dietary remedies work in treating depression?

While most people dealing with depression are going to rely on conventional antidepressant medication, we are seeing a greater push in recent years toward more "natural alternatives," including the use of complementary and alternative medicine, as well as herbal remedies for mood problems. Though over 70 percent of the world's population continues to rely on these herbal remedies, most health care professionals remain skeptical about how effective they actually are.

Among the reasons for the popularity of herbal remedies is the belief that they are healthier than prescription medications since they contain all "natural" ingredients. Unfortunately, because many of these remedies aren't monitored by regulating agencies such as the U.S. Food and Drug Administration (FDA), it's hard to tell how the remedies have been prepared and whether they contain potentially harmful ingredients. Though side effects resulting from use of these herbal remedies and their interactions with other drugs are relatively rare, problems have been known to develop. This is why anyone considering herbal remedies to treat their depression should seek medical advice first.

Some of the most popular herbal remedies currently available are as follows:

> St. John's Wort *(Hypericum perforatum)*: Extracted from the flower of the St. John's Wort plant native to different parts of Europe and Asia, Hypericum has been used for centuries by medical doctors and apothecaries for treating mild to moderate depression. One of the active components of Hypericum, hypericin, appears to reduce serotonin receptor density and may also dampen the production of cortisol by acting on the body's hormonal system. Another active ingredient, hyperforin, seems to inhibit the reuptake of serotonin, norepinephrine, and acetylcholine, though researchers are still not clear about the mechanisms involved.

While most commercial compounds of Hypericum are high in either hypericin or hyperforin, the actual amount of active ingredients can vary widely since herbal medications aren't standardized in the way that prescription medications are. Also, no research data is currently available showing the actual clinical benefits of the different brands on the market.

Research studies comparing Hypericum to placebos tend to show that it is reasonably effective in treating some symptoms of depression. Still, the results of many of these studies have been inconsistent, possibly due to the lack of a standardized form of Hypericum. At present, there is no clear evidence that Hypericum is as effective as prescription antidepressant medications.

People who wish to take Hypericum need to be aware of possible side effects, including a greater sensitivity to ultraviolet radiation and possible interaction with certain kinds of medication. Do not take Hypericum without medical advice.

> Omega-3 Fatty Acids: An active ingredient in certain types of food, fish, nuts, and seeds, omega-3 fatty acids have become popular as a

natural treatment for depression in recent years. This is largely based on research suggesting that the modern Western diet is deficient in these nutrients. On the other hand, people from countries where fish is more widely eaten tend to have a healthier plasma ratio of omega-6 compared to omega-3. These healthier eating habits, coupled with experiencing less stress than is found in Western societies, may lead to fewer problems with inflammation, including cardiovascular disease and mood disorders.

Though the exact mechanism linking omega-3 fatty acids to reduced depression hasn't been identified, researchers have identified potential explanations. For example, administration of omega-3 supplements such as eicosapentaenoic acid (EPA) and docosahexaenoic acid (DHA) can lower plasma norepinephrine levels and may also affect the release of hormones linked to higher stress.

Randomized, placebo-controlled trials using EPA and/or DHA suggests that high doses of omega-3 supplements may have antidepressant effects, though, typically, the dosages required are around fifteen times the current daily levels found in most Western diets. Omega-3 supplements may also help treat postpartum depression and bipolar disorder as well as other conditions such as obsessive-compulsive disorder. Still, most of these studies have small sample sizes, and more research needs to be done.

While omega-3 supplements such as EPA and DHA have few side effects, they should still not be taken without medical advice, especially for people with other medical problems or who are taking medications such as blood thinners.

> SAMe: Also known as adenosylmethionine, SAMe is a molecule that forms naturally in the body and which plays a role in the synthesis of key proteins, hormones, and neurotransmitters. This includes norepinephrine, dopamine, and serotonin. Available by prescription in many parts of Europe for decades as an extremely popular treatment for depression, SAMe is mainly sold as a dietary supplement in North America. This has been changing in recent years, however, and it has become increasingly popular as a natural remedy for depression. Despite reports that SAMe may work even more rapidly than conventional antidepressants, medical researchers have identified potential side effects. These include gastric problems, dry mouth, and sweating. While many people take SAMe along with regular antidepressant treatment, it is important to get medical clearance first. This is particularly true for people who have additional medical problems or who are on different types of medication.

As you can see, there are a number of alternative treatments for depression, and many people who have difficulty trusting conventional medicine may prefer to give them a try. Still, being "natural" doesn't necessarily mean that they are safe to take. Anyone considering one of these alternative remedies should consult with a medical doctor to avoid problems. It is also important to remember that herbal supplements and alternative remedies aren't monitored as carefully as prescription medications are, so potential users should do their homework about which brands are best before trying them.

42. What is cognitive behavioral therapy?

Cognitive behavioral therapy (CBT) is an overall term describing a range of problem-oriented psychotherapy techniques focusing on identifying and changing harmful thoughts and behaviors. Unlike more traditional forms of psychotherapy, CBT clients and their therapists work together in an active partnership to explore the negative thoughts, feelings, and behaviors that can underlie negative thinking and depression.

How these negative beliefs develop often depends on the social and cultural experiences people have growing up and whether there are other accompanying health problems such as chronic pain, social anxiety, or substance abuse. Though CBT tends to focus on current thought patterns and behaviors, people dealing with other mental health issues or early abuse may also explore how these issues may be sabotaging their recovery.

Part of the appeal of CBT is its flexibility. Not only can it be administered either individually or in treatment groups but CBT can also be adapted for use in couples or family therapy or in dealing with clients with special needs. Along with CBT programs for children and adolescents, there are also treatment programs aimed at adults dealing with childhood sexual or physical abuse, domestic violence, or other issues that might trigger chronic depression.

Typically, individual or group CBT sessions can range from forty-five minutes to over an hour per week. Despite having a strong educational component, clients and therapists can also use CBT sessions to exchange information and ideas about how the treatment is going. In a real sense, clients and therapists are working together as part of the therapy process to find real solutions to mental health issues such as depression.

Along with the treatment sessions, clients receive homework assignments with exercises to apply what they learn in treatment. The lessons covered in these assignments can include learning to identify negative thoughts and behaviors that might increase the risk of relapsing, learning coping strategies to deal with potential sources of stress, and learning effective ways of coping with self-defeating thoughts.

While there are different forms of CBT, including dialectic behavior therapy, rational living therapy, rational emotive behavior therapy, cognitive therapy, and rational behavior therapy, they all focus on a series of core principles including functional analysis, behavior modification, and skill training.

Functional analysis involves clients and their therapists working together to explore the clients' own thoughts and beliefs and how they can shape their behavior. Clients are encouraged to talk openly and honestly about their depression and explore the way that their mood issues have impacted their lives. Using techniques such as the Socratic method, clients learn to identify destructive beliefs and thinking patterns by questioning many of the assumptions they have always taken for granted in the past.

In the early stages of treatment, clients use functional analysis to understand the kind of triggers that can lead to problem behaviors and negative thinking. They also gain insights into their self-doubts and the kind of situations that reinforce these negative beliefs. To help this process along, people in therapy are encouraged to keep a cognitive diary in which they record any thoughts or challenges they may have when not in treatment. Diaries are also useful in monitoring their behavior when they are in social situations or when they encounter problems that might lead to backsliding.

Along with functional analysis, clients also receive skill training to unlearn destructive habits and thought patterns and develop healthier alternatives. Using techniques such as cognitive restructuring, substance abusers learn to examine and change the addictive beliefs and automatic thinking patterns that can lead to problem behaviors. Destructive beliefs or automatic thinking patterns can include, "I am not attractive/popular enough to socialize with other people," "They are laughing at me," or "Nobody cares about me."

While reinforcing negative thinking, these automatic beliefs may also reflect how users view themselves or the world in general. Having a poor opinion of their own self-worth, their current circumstances, or their family situation can also feed into intensive brooding, not to mention sabotage any attempt at helping themselves. These beliefs also grow and change over time as users become increasingly pessimistic about the possibility of making a real change.

Automatic beliefs are often based on cognitive distortions or errors in thinking people often make. These include all or nothing thinking, (seeing situations in black or white terms), overgeneralizations (viewing any setback as a sign that change is impossible), mental filtering to focus only on the negative, or jumping to conclusions about the way they view the world.

As part of their skill training, clients are taught how to incorporate these positive thought patterns into their daily life and to develop positive behavior patterns that can defeat the old patterns that encourage self-doubt and negative thinking. Over the course of treatment, clients can also engage in role-play and behavioral rehearsal to learn more positive ways of thinking and behaving in situations that might help them to be more self-assertive. This also allows them to practice their new skills and become more comfortable in making them a part of their daily routine.

Other skills that can be learned during CBT sessions include relaxation training, problem-solving training, stress inoculation, guided imagery, assertiveness training, and mindfulness training (more on that in Question 43).

Behavior modification (also known as contingency management) focuses on making positive changes in how a client behaves on a daily basis. This is often based on principles of operant conditioning by using specific rewards to reinforce positive behavior (such as avoiding brooding behavior or isolation). There are different kinds of rewards that can be used including gift vouchers, spending time with friends or family, or some other form of recognition that reinforce the gains being made. This allows clients attending treatment to make real changes to their daily routines that can continue long after the treatment program has ended.

Since CBT is a short-term treatment approach, most treatment programs are time limited (having a fixed ending date after a set number of treatment sessions). As a result, clients are encouraged to plan how they will apply what they have learned once the treatment has ended. This makes CBT quite different from more traditional approaches which are more open ended.

Research studies have demonstrated the effectiveness of CBT in the treatment of substance abuse, depression, eating disorders, and other mental health problems. Large-scale studies of CBT in the treatment of depression and other mood disorders have found it to be highly effective for many people. Combining CBT with other treatment approaches such as antidepressant medication can be particularly useful in steering clients toward a healthier lifestyle.

43. What is mindfulness therapy?

Originally a part of Buddhist teachings, mindfulness deals with the process of focusing attention on the here and now without worrying about past experiences or having fears about the future. Among the different mindfulness-based treatment approaches available are mindfulness-based cognitive therapy (MBCT), mindfulness-based stress reduction (MBSR), and mindful-oriented recovery enhancement (MORE). For that matter, there are also a growing number of "third-wave" behavioral treatments that have included mindfulness training as modules in their programs. These include acceptance and commitment therapy (ACT) and dialectical behavior therapy (DBT).

Despite the numerous different approaches using mindfulness training, they all involve the use of meditation, guided imagery, or mental visualization exercises to allow people to focus on those specific thoughts, physical sensations, and desires that might be undermining their mental or physical health. This means that participants can learn how to take in and accept all incoming thoughts and feelings without resorting to automatic thoughts and beliefs that might be destructive. Also, much like with CBT, participants are given regular homework assignments so that they can regularly practice what they learn in the treatment sessions. This allows them to become more comfortable with the techniques as well as use them on a daily basis.

Now widely used in the treatment of a range of mental health issues such as depression, stress, and social anxiety, mindfulness training represents one of the most promising approaches for people to come to terms with emotional issues and negative thinking.

For people dealing with depression, mindfulness training can be especially useful in accepting negative emotions and the self-talk that can influence mood. Since people have an innate need to avoid painful situations and seek out pleasurable sensations, dealing with cravings is a perpetual problem for substance abusers who might otherwise want to stay clean.

Research looking at the effectiveness of mindfulness-based treatment has shown that it can be especially beneficial in reducing depression and other mood disorders. Researchers examining the effects of mindfulness meditation on brain functioning have found evidence of significantly increased activity in the prefrontal cortex during meditation. This can help with negative self-talk and emotional regulation and can make coping much easier during depressive episodes.

One of the advantages of mindfulness training is the way that it can be combined with other group and individual treatment approaches and even included as part of family or couple therapy. Mindfulness training seems to work especially well when combined with CBT, which can reinforce the benefits this kind of treatment can provide.

A recent research review of nine clinical trials of people with severe depression showed that MBCT helps reduce the risk of relapsing in depression regardless of age, sex, relationship status, or level of education.

Mindfulness-based therapy has also been found to be as effective as medication in many cases, and in one recent study, many of the patients completing a mindfulness therapy program felt confident enough to stop their medication completely.

While mindfulness-based therapy is hardly a cure-all for people dealing with depression, it is a promising treatment tool that is likely to become more widely used in future.

44. What is interpersonal psychotherapy?

Once known as "high contact" therapy, interpersonal psychotherapy (IPT for short) was first developed by psychologists at Yale University as a brief intervention for the treatment of major depression and has since been adapted for a wide range of other mental health issues. Partly based on attachment theory (see Question 21), IPT focus on relieving symptoms by improving the way people interact with family, friends, and peers. One of the central concepts of IPT is that psychological issues such as depression and anxiety occur due to problems in the everyday relationships we all have with the important people in our lives.

People undergoing IPT learn to focus on developing their relationship skills and learning better communication strategies to overcome those conflicts that can lead to emotional distress. The relationship problems that may be explored in IPT usually fall into four categories:

- conflict in relationships leading to tension and distress
- significant life transitions—for example, losing or starting a new job or starting a new school—that can affect how participants may view themselves and others
- unresolved grief and loss
- difficulties in starting or sustaining relationships; this includes identifying the interpersonal shortfalls that can sabotage relationships

With IPT, the first three treatment sessions usually focus on helping participants create a list of all their important relationships as well as identifying the problems they may be experiencing. Based on what is discovered during these early sessions, the therapist then prepares a treatment contract outlining what the therapy is intended to achieve as well as how long the treatment will take. While a standard IPT usually runs from twelve to sixteen treatment sessions, the therapist may well decide that additional sessions will be needed based on the kind of relationship problems that need to be addressed.

Participants are encouraged to examine their important relationships and determine the type of problem they may be experiencing. This allows participants to work with the counselor to decide on what relationship issues they may want to concentrate on in the following sessions.

In the weekly sessions that follow, participants also learn about attachment theory and how it may be used to understand how relationship problems first develop and why the difficulties they may be experiencing keep occurring. They also learn about positive and negative communication strategies that can help or hinder the forming of new relationships or maintaining existing ones.

During the course of these treatment sessions, participants are encouraged to examine past and present relationships to identify what may have led to problems forming. This includes looking at specific interpersonal situations that may have been especially distressing and exploring how they responded to those situations as well as possible alternatives that might have worked better.

One important feature of IPT treatment sessions is the assigning of "homework" that participants can do on their own. These homework assignments help clarify the different skills learned in the treatment programs and allow for additional practice at home.

During the final two or three sessions, the therapist reviews what has been learned and allows the participant to provide feedback about the treatment and the kind of issues that may need to be addressed in future. As with CBT, people who have successfully completed IPT treatment may follow up with maintenance sessions that allow them to review the material presented and practice the skills they have been taught.

Numerous research studies have already demonstrated the value of IPT in the treatment of depression and other mood disorders. Though originally developed for adults with depression, specialized IPT programs have also been developed for adolescents and preadolescents that focus on relationship problems experienced at a younger age.

Much like other treatment programs that are widely available, IPT isn't necessarily suitable for all people who experience depression. Still, it can be highly beneficial in helping them deal with relationship issues and learn to cope better with their mood problems.

45. Who should receive group therapy?

Many people suffering from depression or other mood disorders find group therapy to be extremely valuable in helping them come to terms with their symptoms. Listening to other people share their own stories can help patients in the group feel less isolated. Also, people in the group can develop deep emotional bonds with other group members and help overcome their own issues in the course of treatment. Still, group therapy isn't for everybody and should be used as part of a broader treatment process along with individual counseling sessions.

Any potential group therapy patient needs to be carefully screened to ensure that they benefit from being in a group with other patients. Some patients may not have be comfortable sharing their lives with other group members or may have poor social skills that might lead to them becoming disruptive. Also, socially anxious patients may decide to stay silent without ever participating.

Group therapy patients need to be properly motivated to be part of a treatment group and show proper empathy for what other group members are sharing about their own lives. Most importantly, they need to respect their fellow group members and respect their right to privacy by keeping all information they may learn in the group strictly confidential.

Along with mood-disordered clients who share their stories as part of the group, group therapy sessions can also include sessions looking at different coping strategies such as relaxation training, social skills development, self-confidence building, anger management, and mindfulness training. Though some participants may not feel that this material is immediately helpful to them, the skills they develop in these sessions can be essential in helping them move on with their recovery.

Unfortunately, some group members may feel a need to "compete" with the other patients in the group either through acting as if their problems are more important or else by trying to dominate the group and not giving other patients a chance to contribute. Ideally, the ground rules for participation in the group will be laid down at the beginning, and patients may begin with individual counseling until the therapist decides that they are ready.

For people dealing with depression, there is another issue that needs to be considered. Group members who are feeling suicidal or who have attempted suicide in that past may provide potentially gruesome details, even if they aren't trying to shock the other people in the group. Hearing many of these details can be deeply disturbing for depressed people who are dealing with similar suicidal ideas. This is why therapists first need to work with their patients on an individual basis to ensure they are ready to cope with the intensity that can often occur in group therapy sessions.

By attending group therapy sessions on a regular basis, participants can develop a sense of hope at seeing how others have succeeded in overcoming problems very similar to what they are going through. Also, by imitating the examples provided by the therapist and other group members, they can learn to understand themselves better and develop real alternatives that can make coping easier.

46. What can parents do to help children who are depressed?

It seems almost inevitable that parents blame themselves whenever one of their children develops a mood disorder. Not only do they wonder if their parenting was somehow responsible for it but they may also feel guilty over missing warning signs that might have alerted them sooner that something was wrong. Unfortunately, many parents may choose to ignore these symptoms for as long as possible in the hope that their child might "snap out of it." But depression doesn't go away if it is ignored.

For any parent who wants to find the right help for a depressed child, the first step is always to recognize that something is wrong and become willing to take action. This means accepting a child's mood problems as a challenge that needs to be overcome. It also means educating themselves about depression, its causes, and possible treatment options. Just as importantly, they need to be realistic about any expectations they might have about how quickly a treatment will work. Overcoming depression isn't something that can happen overnight, and parents need to work together with their child's therapist to ensure the best possible care.

Parents also need to set clear boundaries for their depressed child, but again, these have to be reasonable boundaries. This includes a willingness to get tough whenever their child acts out in any way and laying down ground rules that even depressed children should be expected to follow. Injecting a sense of structure into a child's life can teach them to monitor their own behavior.

Since people who are depressed often feel moody and unloved, making certain that they know that their parents care about them can be an essential part of providing the right kind of support. This includes avoiding blanket statements such as "I know how you feel" (chances are, you don't). Be prepared to sit down with them and simply listen to what they have to say.

Parents also need to avoid giving advice (which, admittedly, is a hard habit for mothers and fathers to break). While people with depression may want honest feedback at times, advice shouldn't be forced onto them. If they are prepared to listen, they will.

Once a depressed child begins treatment, the first few weeks are going to be especially crucial. Parents need to provide encouragement and to be patient. For many people in treatment, whether as adults or adolescents, the temptation to simply give up is going to be particularly strong at first. Progress isn't going to come as fast as they might have originally hoped, and as a result, they may assume that the treatment isn't working and that the depression won't go away.

At the same time, parents need to monitor their children to ensure that they keep taking medication or attend treatment as needed. All too frequently, particularly for people experiencing depression for the first time, many who find their mood lifting may decide that they have recovered and no longer need treatment. Parents and therapists need to work together to reinforce the importance of continuing the treatment and be willing to be a part of the treatment process.

Simply knowing that their parents are supportive and accepting may play a critical role in patients learning how to deal with depression.

47. Can online support groups help with depression?

For many depressed people who want to attend treatment, the problem of finding treatment programs can be difficult, especially if they live in a small community where certain programs may not be available. Anyone attending treatment for the first time may also feel reluctant to become part of a treatment group where they would be expected to talk about their emotional problems and share many of their most intimate secrets with people they have never met before.

As a result, many people with depression may be tempted to go online and take advantage of one of the numerous Internet support groups already available. Not only would this allow them to stay anonymous but these groups are usually free and can be accessed at any time of the day or night.

But how effective are these online groups when compared to in-person treatment programs when it comes to treating depression? Research looking at Internet-based cognitive behavioral therapy (iCBT) suggests that it can be as effective as traditional in-person treatment programs in treating depression. Still, much of this research is in the very early stage, and many more studies need to be done to determine whether this kind of online help can become more widely used.

Despite the appeal of online, often anonymous treatment programming, there are drawbacks as well. Since online groups often allow people to participate without revealing their identity, this removes much of the emotional connection that those participating in face-to-face meetings would experience. Meeting in-person also allows depressed patients to relearn how to communicate honestly and avoid the impulse to lie when being asked uncomfortable questions. In-person group members also learn to form strong emotional bonds with fellow group members and their therapist, something that can be extremely important for people who want to open up about secrets they might not otherwise share. With online counseling, on the other hand, many of the benefits of in-person treatment are often lacking.

Despite the disadvantages of online treatment programs, there is no disputing that they are becoming much more popular. Not only are there far more options available online than most people are likely to find in their own community, but joining an online group is far easier than finding an in-person treatment program. Considering that many programs may not be covered by standard health plans or receive government support, that also adds to its appeal.

Though online treatment is becoming increasingly popular, in-person treatment will continue to be available for people who need something more comprehensive to overcome depression. People seeking treatment should be able to investigate a wide range of treatment options. This can mean using online resources in supplementing the help that can come from conventional treatment, though it should never replace it completely.

If you are considering online treatment groups, make sure you do your homework to ensure that such treatment is the right choice for you. Most reputable treatment programs are affiliated with national or international organizations that also provide access to local resources as well as other resources that can help. Check the appendix section for some possible online sites to contact.

48. Does the risk of depression ever go away?

In a real sense, this is a loaded question. As we've already seen in previous section, there are always going to be times when we start "feeling the blues." Whether due to grief, disappointment, or the inevitable setbacks that are a part of being human, nobody is going to be happy all the time. For people who have already experienced the often- crippling symptoms of true depression, it's perfectly natural to worry that the depression will return someday and that what seems like an ordinary case of the blues might become something far worse.

While the recidivism rate for major depression is uncomfortably high (50 percent according to recent estimates), this does not mean that someone who has already experienced depression is doomed to relapse at some point. Some people may just be especially vulnerable to depression (due to genetics, other mental health problems, or an abusive relationship, etc.), but they can still learn to move on with their lives without experiencing new episodes.

Even though the risk of relapse will never completely go away, anyone worrying about slipping back into their old self-destructive patterns of thinking and behaving should consider the following:

- First of all, the very act of surviving depression the first time around often means being much stronger as a result. In writing about his own battle with depression, author William Styron described it as being "mysterious in its coming, mysterious in its going, the affliction runs its course, and one finds peace." Resilience, which is usually defined as the ability to recover quickly from adversity, is a quality that is often found in trauma survivors. But it can also be seen in people who have faced depression and bounced back from it. Knowing that depression *can* be overcome is an essential part of surviving when the dark times return.

- Treatment programs such as CBT and IPT involve the teaching of basic coping skills that can be used to deal with new depressive episodes as they arise. This includes learning to control negative ruminations, maintaining a positive mind-set, and resolving interpersonal problems before they become toxic. Continue practicing these skills even after the treatment ends so that they can be used whenever the need arises.

- But these skills aren't simply for dealing with depression. We all encounter major life problems that can seem hopeless at times. Skills such as muscle relaxation, stress management, and cognitive restructuring can boost our general ability to cope with these new crises as they occur.

- People who have successfully completed treatment for depression already have a support network in place that they can use if they find themselves relapsing. This can include mental health professionals, family physician, local support groups, and family members who have been supportive in the past. Don't be afraid to use these resources as needed.

- Perhaps most importantly of all, do your best to maintain a hopeful outlook. That may seem impossible at times, especially if you're dealing with a traumatic loss or facing a life crisis, but always remember that "this too shall pass."

While the risk of further depression will never go away completely, it is still possible to deal with it as it comes and enjoy life to the fullest. We will explore this a little further in Question 50.

49. How effective are awareness campaigns in helping people who are depressed?

Perhaps more than ever before, we are seeing numerous awareness campaigns aimed at educating people about depression and suicide. For example, the National Alliance on Mental Illness (NAMI) sponsors the National Anxiety and Depression Week as part of Mental Health Month each May as well as Suicide Prevention Awareness Month each September. Along with hosting awareness events nationwide to help combat the stigma surrounding depression and suicide, NAMI and participating groups also provide online resources allowing vulnerable people to learn more about treatment options and to contact therapists in their area. Among the different awareness events organized by NAMI are the annual 5K NAMI-Walks held each May for fundraising and to promote public participation as well as the CureStigma campaign held at different times of the year.

Similar awareness campaigns occur each year in numerous other countries as well. In the United Kingdom, for example, there have been popular programs such as You in Mind, the Defeat Depression, and Changing Minds campaigns to help fight depression, suicide, and mental illness. In Australia and New Zealand, there have been campaigns such as beyondblue; Like Minds, Like Mine; and the Community Awareness Program over the past few decades. Along with these national campaigns, there have also been international ones sponsored by the World Health Organization (WHO) as part of World Health Day. Under the WHO, new awareness campaigns have been held in many developing nations to help combat the terrible stigma surrounding depression and to encourage better mental health care.

But how effective are awareness campaigns in changing attitudes about depression and mental illness and in reducing suicide rates? While numerous research studies looking at national programs such as NAMI's mental health campaigns suggest that they can be effective, comparing different programs is often difficult. A 2009 study examining fifteen programs in eight different countries over a twenty-year period (1987–2007) suggests that the benefits of these programs often depends on how long the programs run and what the programs are intended to accomplish.

For example, many of these programs were extremely short term (often involving only a single television program) with very little follow-up to see if they actually changed attitudes. The most effective programs tended to be much more comprehensive with nationwide coverage and an extensive media campaign that could be repeated on a yearly basis. This ensures that the message these campaigns are intended to deliver reach as many people as possible.

In general, public awareness and information programs about suicide or depression do appear to improve knowledge and awareness of mental illness in the population, at least in the short term. Campaigns can also be effective in teaching "gatekeepers" such as doctors and nurses about depression and suicide and make them better able to inform patients about treatment resources and identify people who might be at risk.

As for whether these awareness campaigns actually reduce suicide rates or encourage more people to seek treatment, the results tend to be mixed. While some programs do appear to make people in need more likely to reach out for help, it's often difficult to tell whether they actually discourage people from attempting suicide. While some research studies show an increase in calls to suicide hotlines following media campaigns, this effect is usually temporary. As a result, public exposure campaigns seem to work best when there is repeated exposure (such as with annual campaigns) since this helps reinforce the message they are trying to get across.

While public awareness campaigns aren't going to eliminate depression and reduce suicide on their own, they can help people overcome many of the misconceptions that can interfere with them getting help. They can also make the general public more aware of how to identify friends and family members who might be at risk and help them get treatment before it's too late.

50. Can people who have been depressed learn to move on with their lives?

While treatment and support from health care professionals, family, and friends can play a key role in helping people with depression get better, it's ultimately up to them to take charge of their emotional well-being and learn to move on; that means developing the kind of healthy habits that can boost resilience and coping with mood changes as they occur.

And they *will* occur again at some point or other. We all have "dark days" due to setbacks or disappointments that can bring back the symptoms of depression, if only temporarily. For those who have already experienced depression and who are feeling as if their symptoms are returning, here are some commonsense things you can do to help yourself as you seek treatment:

- Don't neglect your physical health. Though people who are feeling despondent often feel apathetic as well, it is essential that they take care of their physical needs as well. This means trying to get a good night's sleep (even if you find yourself resisting this); practice good sleep hygiene. It's also important to exercise regularly and stay as active as possible.
- Make sure you eat regularly even if you lose your appetite. Take a multivitamin tablet each day to avoid nutritional problems. If you find yourself losing weight too rapidly, see your doctor immediately.
- Follow all recommended treatment. If you are on medication, keep taking it as prescribed. Discontinuing medication abruptly can be extremely dangerous, even if you feel it isn't working. Also, if you have gone through psychotherapy, use the techniques you have learned to help get your mood under control. See your doctor if your current treatment isn't working.
- Join a support group. If you have already been in treatment, you likely already know where to go to find individual or group counseling in your community. You can also try online resources, including chat rooms or online group support such as the ones listed in the appendix.
- Rely on your family and friends for help. Many depressed people who experience a relapse may be reluctant to tell family or friends what is happening because they don't want to be a burden or they are afraid of being rejected. More likely than not, the people in your life will already be aware that something is wrong and want to help.
- Keep a journal. Many people dealing with depression find that writing down what they are thinking on a daily basis can help them keep a clear head.
- Be careful with your computer. Not only can regular use of social media sites such as Facebook add to your depression, but many depressed people are especially vulnerable to using online sites as a way of shutting out the real world.
- Avoid making life-altering decisions. Depression has a way of distorting judgment, and more often than not, you are going to end up regretting making hasty decisions that will likely haunt you later on.
- Don't blame yourself for feeling depressed. Not only are depressed people plagued with self-doubts but their self-esteem plummets as

well. Hold onto hope and accept that what you're going through will pass eventually.

- And finally, and most importantly, seek help immediately if you are feeling suicidal or have difficulty controlling thoughts of self-harm.

Continue taking care of yourself and recognize that your depression can be controlled. Even if you dread the thought of going through the whole treatment process again, the knowledge that depressive episodes pass with time can make the future seem a little brighter.

Case Studies

Case 1: David

When David's older brother, Gary, died in a car accident, it seemed as if the world had come to an end. All his life, David had looked up to Gary and counted on him for help whenever he needed it. When he turned nineteen, David was even planning to go to the same college that Gary was attending just to have a chance to see his brother on campus from time to time.

When his parents told him the news about Gary's death, David had refused to believe it at first. He even insisted that he could feel Gary's presence in his room and could hear his voice at times, something that seemed to pass quickly enough though the emotional numbness he began showing made his parents worry even more about his mental state.

Though David's parents were dealing with their own emotions following Gary's death, they saw that David was taking it especially hard. They even offered to arrange grief counseling that the entire family could attend. Increasingly moody since Gary's death, David snapped that he didn't need counseling though his parents could see that he was going into a decline.

Not only was he cutting class more frequently, but he was often up at night, and his parents could hear him wandering through the house early in the morning. Whenever they tried to talk to him about this, however, he would just lash out at them. According to his friends, David was much more aggressive at school and was on the verge of being suspended if his behavior failed to improve.

David's parents became even more alarmed when his mother discovered that he had begun cutting himself though he had been careful not to require a visit to the hospital (so far). He also began sneaking alcohol from the liquor cabinet that his parents kept for visitors, and his mother became alarmed by the empty bottles in David's room. When they confronted him about his drinking, he just lashed out at them over invading his privacy.

Finally, following an incident at school where he punched a fellow student, David was suspended, and his parents decided to take matters into their own hands. After consulting with a counselor recommended by their family doctor, they arranged for him to start attending a grief support group being held at a local community center. While David refused at first, his parents ordered him to attend as a condition of continuing to live under their roof. Though they were unhappy to have to get tough with their son, they knew how much he needed to talk to someone about what he was going through.

Before the group began, however, David received a phone call from Laura, one of the groups' facilitators, who helped explain what the group was all about and what would be expected of him. The group was aimed at young people who were the same age as David, all of whom were dealing with grief and loss. While David had been afraid that he would be expected to "spill his guts" to total strangers, Laura made it clear to him that he wouldn't be made to do anything that made him uncomfortable and that it was perfectly fine just to sit and listen for a while. Based on what Laura told him, David decided to give the group a try.

Though David was reluctant to speak at first, he became more comfortable after hearing each group member share his or her story, Since all of them had dealt with a similar loss, David decided to open up about losing his brother. Over the next few weeks, he began to form a bond with the other group members since he felt they knew what he was feeling. He also admitted to feeling alienated from his parents and his friends who kept saying the wrong thing or otherwise making it clear that they didn't really understand what he was going through.

Just as importantly, David was able to provide support for other group members and show them that they were not alone. This helped him recognize that grief was a perfectly normal reaction to sudden loss and provided him with practical tips on how to handle the changes resulting from Gary's death as well as learn how to move on with his own life.

While he still misses his brother and likely always will, David has managed to pull back from his depression and is managing his school and home life a little better. He continues to attend the group and has even helped facilitate a few meetings. So far, so good.

Analysis

Though dealing with the loss of a parent, sibling, or close friend is something that many young people will experience at some point, this kind of bereavement can also make them much more susceptible to depression. Since not all young people are going to react to grief in quite the same way, it's hard to anticipate how this kind of loss will affect them. While denial, anger, sadness, guilt, and anxiety are all perfectly normal reactions to grief, young people may try to keep these feeling to themselves. There are still signs that parents and teachers can watch for in children and adolescents dealing with loss, however. They include: irritability, social withdrawal, poor performance in school, sleep and appetite problems, aggressiveness, and a tendency toward emotional outbursts. There may also be guilt feelings if they feel responsible for the death by somehow having failed to stop it from happening. They may also feel anxious about the possibility of someone else in their life dying as well. Though not every community will have a group program for young people dealing with grief and loss, peer counseling still can be a valuable resource. By learning how to mourn effectively as well as learning how to cope with feelings of depression stemming from grief, young people can move on with their lives as well as become more resilient with time.

Case 2: Alexa

Fifteen-year-old Alexa has been arguing more frequently with her mother over the past nine months. Alexa had always been a moody child (especially following her parents' divorce) though never to the point of needing counseling. But her mother has become more worried about the changes she is seeing in her daughter and the growing changes in her mood. On one occasion, the argument became so severe that Alexa left the house and stayed away for twelve hours. When her mother asked where she had been, Alexa flatly refused to say. Along with her anger issues, Alexa also seems to have a problem with her self-image and insists that she is unattractive no matter what she wears. Not only is her negative mood affecting her relationship with her mother but she has also alienated the few friends she once had, and her teachers are reporting problems in school, including cutting classes and failing to hand in assignments. When her mother tried to get Alexa to attend counseling with her, she stated that everything was hopeless and nothing would ever get better in the future.

Alexa's mother became even more alarmed when she realized that her daughter was cutting herself. Though the scars were mostly confined to Alexa's wrists (which she kept concealed with long-sleeved shirts and sweaters), her mother soon realized that the self-cutting was becoming much more frequent and often deep enough to require a trip to the emergency room for stitches. Realizing that Alexa was too depressed to ask for help on her own, the mother began attending a support group for parents of children with emotional problems and, while there, began learning of the different programs available in their area that might help her daughter.

Finally, when the self-cutting became more severe, the mother had no choice but to give Alexa an ultimatum: either attend counseling or be sent to an inpatient program due to her suicidal behavior. Though Alexa was furious with her mother who she felt was betraying her, she finally agreed to attend one-to-one counseling at a local clinic. She also agreed to begin taking antidepressant medication (which her mother carefully monitored to ensure that Alexa was actually swallowing the pills).

Treatment was rocky from the start since Alexa had been forced to attend rather than being allowed to choose for herself. Because she was so antagonistic, the counselor made the decision to see her individually rather than put her in the regular group program.

During the first few episodes, Alexa did everything in her power to show that she didn't want to be in treatment. While her mother made certain that she attended every treatment session (despite the various excuses she came up with), getting Alexa to participate and do the homework assignments was especially difficult. Still, there was some progress as Alexa slowly accepted that the therapist was just trying to help.

The real breakthrough came when Alexa's mother attended some of the therapy sessions. This allowed the two of them to interact more frequently and also gave Alexa the opportunity to work through some of her resentment at being forced to attend treatment. Alexa also realized how worried her mother was about her symptoms and her willingness to help find a solution.

As she came to accept the treatment process, Alexa began doing the homework assignments and to stop shutting her mother out. Also, the medication she was taking was helping her to sleep through the night and keep her mood under control a little more than before. Though the medication needed to be carefully monitored by Alexa's doctor, the few side effects she experienced seemed manageable.

Over the course of the treatment sessions, both Alexa's mother and her therapist were encouraged by the progress she appeared to be making. The self-cutting had stopped, and Alexa was eating more regularly. Despite the progress being made, there were still setbacks along the way that jeopardized the treatment she was receiving. She was distressed by conflicts at school, especially in dealing with others her age who targeted her for being in counseling and accused her of being crazy. As a result of these pressures, Alexa threatened to begin self-cutting again.

After a discussion between Alexa's mother and her therapist, they decided to place her in the weekly support group. Despite her mother's concern that Alexa might not be ready for the group, the therapist suggested that allowing her to interact with other clients her age who were going through similar problems would allow Alexa to work on her social skills, especially considering how isolated she had become over the previous year.

While the group sessions are still ongoing, things are looking more hopeful for Alexa. Along with learning how to be more resilient in how she interacts with others, she has learned better coping strategies and has become more social. Along with the new friends she made in the group, she also resumed her relationship with some of her old friends. Though it is likely too soon to treat her as a success story, her mother is feeling more optimistic as well, and their relationship has definitely become stronger as well.

Analysis

For many young people like Alexa, the road to recovery is often rocky. Not only is there no magic cure but they are also often unwilling to enter into therapy due to the stigma that often surrounds depression and other mood disorders. When starting cognitive behavioral psychotherapy (CBT) or some other form of counseling, the therapist often needs to assess whether their young client is capable of forming a good therapeutic relationship. Whether due to problems with emotional maturity or because their depression is too severe, many young people may find themselves unable to handle being in therapy. They may also lack the confidence to open up about what they are feeling. This often leads to them either skipping treatment sessions, being disruptive during the therapy sessions, or simply refusing to interact at all. If the sessions continue to be unproductive, the therapist will need to see whether antidepressant medication can help and also work with parents and other professionals involved to come up with new treatment goals. It may also be necessary to stop the treatment entirely until the client becomes more receptive.

Fortunately in Alexa's case, her medication, as well as the emotional support she was receiving from her mother, helped make her more receptive to the individual counseling, and later the group treatment. Also, through regular review sessions with her therapist, she was able to understand the different ways that she was undermining her own recovery. As her therapeutic journey continued, she learned to become a full partner in the treatment process and learned how to cope with her symptoms. This, in turn, helped her to understand that she wasn't as helpless as she believed and could take control of her life.

Case 3: Adele

Adele is a fifty-two-year-old office administrator who recently went on sick leave due to problems stemming from depression. She was married for the second time two years earlier and denied any problems with her husband. Her three children from her first marriage are all living on their own, and she remains on good terms with them though she avoids talking about her first husband, their father, which still generates some family tension. The marriage had ended bitterly after twenty years, and she continues to have emotional issues as a result though she denied it was contributing to her current depression problems.

Though her children are well aware that their father had been an alcoholic, Adele had never told them about the domestic abuse she had endured in the final years of the marriage (the children had already left home by that point). As a result, she still experiences some posttraumatic symptoms, including occasional nightmares, and avoids talking about her first husband as a result. This has also influenced her relationship with her second husband though she has been careful to avoid opening up to him about her experiences.

While Adele had two previous episodes of depression (once after her marriage ended and the second not long after remarrying), she had responded well to treatment with antidepressant medication and had not been on any medication when her new symptoms began. The trigger for her latest episode of depression stems from her daughter's recent hospitalization for breast cancer, something that runs in her family though Adele had never had any problems. While her daughter is responding well to treatment, it has been a long and difficult recovery, and Adele has been experiencing significant problems acting as her daughter's main caregiver.

Among the symptoms that Adele is currently reporting are lack of energy, sadness (particularly when reminded of her daughter's condition), inability to enjoy many of her regular hobbies such as gardening, and occasional suicidal thoughts. She is under the care of the same psychiatrist she saw during her previous depressive episodes and has also begun taking a newer antidepressant, as the one she had formerly used had some side effects that made her uncomfortable.

Still, while Adele is open to taking medication, she continues to resist attending supportive counseling despite the emotional problems she is facing, both in terms of her daughter's serious health issues and her reluctance to talk about the domestic problems that ended her first marriage. When her husband suggested joint counseling, Adele became agitated and accused him of using the counseling as an excuse to end their marriage.

Finally, after talking with family members and her husband, Adele opened up slightly about how helpless her first husband had made her feel and how her daughter's cancer had brought those feelings back. While she asked her doctor for stronger medication, the doctor suggested that Adele attend counseling as well since the medication alone wasn't controlling her symptoms as well as before.

Following a recommendation made by her doctor, Adele began seeing a therapist who, based on the initial sessions they had together, diagnosed her with major depressive disorder. While some of her symptoms also suggested an anxiety disorder, the therapist outlined the different treatment options available to her, including CBT. They also went over the specific treatment goals that would be covered during the first weeks of treatment and what would be expected of Adele if she wanted to get better.

During the course of this treatment, they explored the kind of automatic beliefs Adele had that were reinforcing her sense of helplessness, both in terms of what she went through with her first husband and her frustration at not being able to help her daughter. The therapist worked closely with Adele to help her understand how these beliefs were making her feel trapped and helpless and to learn more positive coping strategies to deal with the stress she was facing. This included relaxation training, cognitive restructuring, and stress inoculation training, all of which can be important tools in controlling the sense of helplessness that can lead to depression.

While Adele's treatment sessions are still ongoing, she is feeling less pressured and more in control. Along with spending more time with her husband, she is also taking a more proactive role in her daughter's treatment, including working closely with her therapists and making her daughter stick to her chemotherapy regimen. Adele continues to get depressed, but she recognizes that she has a strong support network in place and is more confident about her ability to deal with new life problems as they arise.

Analysis

Studies have long shown that adult survivors of abuse are especially vulnerable to depression. This can include childhood physical and sexual abuse as well as domestic violence, all of which can leave victims feeling as if they have no control over their lives and which can reinforce the kind of automatic thinking commonly seen in depression and anxiety. Even for women who have moved on with new relationships, the sense of helplessness can recur whenever they are faced with some new crisis (including serious health problems developing in a child). Such crises often make women feel as if they are caught in a desperate cycle of new problems that seem to sabotage their lives. Even with the support of family and friends, it is often essential that women like Adele seek out treatment as soon as possible. Not only can a trained counselor provide needed support but can also help them become more aware about how depression and abuse are often related. There are different counseling options available depending on the kind of special needs that clients might have and may include individual or group treatment sessions. The ultimate goal of such treatment is to help clients take control of their lives and learn more effective ways of coping with new life crises as they occur. Recruiting family members or friends as co-therapists can also play an important role in recovery as well as in building up the kind of support network that can make help with future depressive episodes.

Case 4: Laura

Laura is a twenty-six-year old mother who is currently pregnant with her second child. While she experienced postpartum depression after her daughter was born three years earlier, she managed to get over eventually without the need for any formal treatment. This time around, however, seems much worse. Not only is she having more severe pregnancy symptoms but her daughter is also making more demands on her time. As for her husband, he is working full time, and Laura resents that he isn't doing what she considered to be his fair share of caring for their daughter.

Lately, she's been feeling much more despondent and has more trouble finding the energy to do anything but sit and feel unloved. She is also eating much less than she is supposed to at this stage of her pregnancy, something that both her doctor and husband have warned her about. What makes Laura more agitated than ever is recognizing that her old postpartum symptoms seem to be returning, and the thought of having to go through what she experienced the last time is making her more upset than ever.

Her first pregnancy had required a C-section due to unexpected complications that had left her terrified for her baby. She had found the whole experience traumatic and had experienced panic attacks even after taking her baby home. The panic attacks faded with time, but the depression lasted for months, something that she was terrified of going through a second time. She also knows that she can't take any medication while pregnant, so she is trying to "tough it out" without telling anyone what she is feeling.

This first experience with postpartum depression had left her completely unprepared since she hadn't known much about it. Even her birthing class didn't have any information to prepare new mothers, and there was almost nothing about it in the handouts that the nurses at the maternity ward had given her. Though she had found some information online on sites such as postpartumprogress.com, the flashbacks and other trauma symptoms she was experiencing made her feel that the depression would be even worse this time around.

Even more alarming for her were the suicidal thoughts that seemed to hit whenever she was feeling particularly vulnerable. This is what led her to talk to her doctor about what was happening. While the doctor could not prescribe antidepressant medication since she was still breastfeeding, she did refer Laura to a psychologist who often dealt with postpartum depression.

After the first few sessions, the therapist arranged for Laura's husband to attend joint counseling to get him more involved in her treatment. Laura was reluctant about this, especially since she and her husband had been experiencing relationship problems that had been made worse by her depression, but eventually agreed. Her husband, Bob, had difficulty as well, especially since he was afraid of saying anything that might upset Laura further. As the sessions continued, both Laura and Bob learned more about postpartum depression and the triggers that were contributing to Laura's depression as well as their relationship issues.

During the sessions, which continued even after Laura gave birth to her son, she became more open with Bob, including being able to communicate her feelings to him, something that she had been afraid to do in the past. Not only did this make her feel less alone but she and her husband also agreed to share childcare duties more evenly, which relieved some of her stress. She was also able to open up about how bad the depression had been the first time around, something she had never told him before (though he admitted to being aware of it).

While Laura still experiences occasional episodes of depression, she is much more optimistic about the future. Also, her relationship with her husband and children has improved immensely, and she has become much more socially active and is trying to get back to her regular life as much as possible. She is also determined to do something to boost awareness of postpartum depression. Along with getting in touch with the local branch of Postpartum Support International, she also helped organize a Climb Out of the Darkness walk in her community. Though it is starting out small, she is hoping to make it an annual event and to encourage more people to attend. She is also making sure that the maternity ward at her local hospital provides more comprehensive information about postpartum depression, including numbers to contact for people who want more information.

Analysis

While having a baby is often seen as a happy time for mothers, the months before and after giving birth can be extremely stressful due to the new responsibilities involved as well as the physical and emotional changes that all women go through. As a result, postpartum depression can be a common problem faced by many new mothers (see Question 15). In fact, women are far more likely to receive mental health counseling during their childbearing years than at any other time in their lives. Even though many women may be reluctant to admit to what they are experiencing (especially if they view their symptoms as being fairly mild), postpartum depression should not be left untreated, especially if the symptoms don't seem to be going away. As postpartum depression is becoming more widely recognized, it is becoming common practice for health care professionals to screen new mothers for symptoms of depression and for hospital maternity wards to provide new parents with educational brochures on how to get help when needed. Also, though postpartum depression was once viewed as a problem that affected the mother alone, therapists now recognize that the kind of relationship mothers have with their partners and other family members can play a critical role in developing symptoms. For this reason, couples and family counseling can be extremely valuable in helping mothers deal with their symptoms and prevent relapses during later pregnancies. While women like Laura may be reluctant to speak out about what they are feeling out of fear of being considered crazy, it is only through speaking out that help becomes possible.

Case 5: Christopher

Since Christopher often regarded himself as a survivor due to the physical abuse that he endured while growing up in the foster system, it came as a surprise to him that he began experiencing symptoms of depression years later.

At twenty-four years of age, Christopher was working full time and going to school at night to finish high school. He was also in a good relationship though he found himself feeling more pessimistic about his future despite all the positives in his life. He certainly remembered how depressed he got as a foster child and how he would resort to drinking and whatever drugs he could get to relieve his moodiness. Though he has been clean for years, he finds himself feeling less confident about his ability to handle the adult responsibilities he thought he was prepared for. While he tries to hide his moodiness as much as possible, his girlfriend is noticing the change and how he has become more irritable and impatient. He is also losing weight since he is eating much less than usual though, again, he has been trying to keep this hidden from anyone who might notice.

To make things worse, his moodiness is affecting his relationship with his employer and coworkers, and he has recently received a negative performance review as a result. Suddenly, it seems harder than ever to keep things together, and Christopher feels that he is about to snap. But it was only after his girlfriend, Beth, noticed the red marks on his hands (he had been punching walls in his apartment to relieve stress) that he finally opened up to her about what was happening to him.

Not only was Beth sympathetic (which he hadn't been expecting) but she was also candid about her own fight with depression years earlier and urged Christopher to attend treatment at the same place she had attended. Given his past experience with youth counselors while he was still in the foster system, Christopher was convinced that treatment would be a waste of time. Still, with all the setbacks in his life recently, he was afraid that his relationship with Beth would end if he didn't at least give it a try.

When Beth took him to the counseling center, Christopher was put off by the appearance of the place and the thought of having to open up to a total stranger. When Beth introduced him to the counselor she had worked with years earlier, the counselor explained the procedure that all new clients would have to go through, including an intake interview and completing some psychological tests to explore the kind of treatment he might need.

During the intake, Christopher was able to open up about the different symptoms he was experiencing (including the wall punching), and the counselor carefully outlined the treatment options available to him. This included individual counseling to help him work through some of the anger he was still feeling about how he had been treated in the foster system as well as the maladaptive coping strategies that had helped him "keep his cool" back then but which were not working for him as an adult.

The counselor also helped him identify the goals that he would be working toward in treatment, including exploring some of the triggers that brought on his episodes of depression as well as dealing with the automatic beliefs that were sabotaging him in his daily life. This included his own fears about whether he would ever be able to have a normal life or whether his time in foster care had permanently damaged his ability to be in a relationship. This also meant exploring his relationship with Beth, someone he viewed as being "much too good for him" and his fear of losing what he regarded as the first real relationship he had ever had.

Along with the individual counseling sessions, Christopher's counselor also suggested that he join the treatment group to gain a better perspective on how different people coped with the kind of problems he was experiencing. Since many of the others in the group were also former foster children who had faced similar abuse in the past, this allowed Christopher to understand that his problems were far from unique. Also, by sharing his experiences with the group, he was able to overcome a lot of his old anger and help defuse the automatic thoughts that led to depression.

Christopher continues to have depressive episodes, but he is functioning better at work and is almost finished with his high school upgrading. He is also more confident about his relationship with Beth and hopes that things will continue to improve between them. In the meantime, his treatment sessions are continuing, and his therapist is optimistic about the progress he has made.

Analysis

For people who experienced abuse as children, the effects of this abuse can persist well into adulthood. This is especially true when dealing with the cumulative effects of repeated abuse over many years. Even as adults, these early experiences are going to shape the way they think, feel, and interact with other people, whether they realize it or not. Along with the trauma stemming from their early abuse, there are also issues with forming poor attachments as children than can affect their relationships as adults. As a result, survivors of childhood abuse can find themselves being adversely affected by the memory of these early traumatic experiences. Research studies have shown that victims of childhood sexual, physical, or emotional abuse often develop maladaptive patterns of dealing with stress that can leave them vulnerable to new stress as it arises. According to the stress sensitization hypothesis, individuals exposed to childhood adversity tend to be much more vulnerable to later problems, including depression and generalized anxiety. Even for people like Chris whose lives appear to be good, the inevitable stress that comes with new challenges and responsibilities can lead to emotional problems that they may not be equipped to handle on their own. While counseling can be effective in helping abuse survivors learn to handle stress and emotional difficulties more effectively, it is still important that they seek treatment as soon as possible. Such counseling can help them learn to be more resilient as well as help to develop support networks, whether family or friends, that can provide them with emotional support as needed.

Glossary

Anhedonia: Defined as the inability to feel pleasure, anhedonia is a common symptom of depression that can take different forms. These include motivational anhedonia (lack of motivation to engage in formerly pleasurable activities) and social anhedonia (inability to feel pleasure from social activities). Anhedonia is often associated with the emotional numbing experienced in mood disorders and trauma.

Antidepressant medications: A class of medications used for the treatment of depressive symptoms. Most antidepressants work by changing the balance of neurotransmitters in the brain that can affect mood and emotions. Different types of antidepressants include selective serotonin uptake inhibitors (SSRIs), atypical antidepressants, tricyclic antidepressants (TCAs), and monamine oxidase inhibitors (MAOIs). Antidepressant medication needs to be closely monitored due to the possibility of side effects as well as interaction effects with other medications.

Apathy: Lack of emotion, interest, or concern. A common symptom in many depressed people, in which they believe that "nothing matters" or that they are unable to make themselves care about things that once concerned them. Often associated with learned helplessness.

Attachment theory: A well-accepted theory that views many behavioral and emotional problems as arising out of attachment difficulties occurring in the critical period between infancy and the age of five. Since a strong attachment needs to form to allow for healthy emotional development, disruptions caused by abuse or neglect can led to emotional insecurity and avoidant behavior.

Attention-deficit hyperactivity disorder (ADHD): A condition characterized by a limited attention and trouble focusing on tasks, impulsive behavior, and difficulty sitting still. While usually diagnosed in children, it can also occur in adults. ADHD can produce symptoms such as insomnia, memory and concentration problems, and mood changes in many people, which may lead to it being misdiagnosed as depression.

Automatic beliefs: Cognitive distortions or errors in thinking that can contribute to depression and other emotional disorders. Different automatic beliefs can include all or nothing thinking, (seeing situations in black or white terms), overgeneralizations (viewing any setback as a sign that change is impossible), mental filtering to focus only on the negative, or jumping to conclusions about the way they view the world.

Behavior modification: Also known as contingency management, this mode of treatment focuses on making positive changes in how a client behaves on a daily basis. Based on principles of operant conditioning, behavioral modification works by using specific rewards to reinforce positive behavior (such as avoiding brooding behavior or isolation).

Behavioral shutdown hypothesis: A recent hypothesis suggesting depression can actually be a healthy coping mechanism under some circumstances since it helps us adapt to extreme situations by reducing activity as much as possible. This kind of shutdown causes people with depression to take time out of their lives to allow for recovery.

Bipolar disorder: A mood disorder similar to depression although symptoms often swing from feeling extremely depressed to feeling manic (i.e., superenergized or on top of the world). A less severe equivalent is cyclothymic disorder.

Chronic fatigue syndrome (CFS): Also known as myalgic encephalomyelitis, this condition can be characterized by symptoms such as concentration and sleep problems, extreme fatigue, and muscle pain. Until fairly recently, CFS was routinely misdiagnosed as depression by medical doctors. Diagnostic testing for this sufferers can prescribe antidepressant medications.

Cognitive behavior therapy for chronic pain (CBT-CP): Developed by therapists at the Veterans Administration for treating injured veterans, CBT-CP teaches patients to manage their chronic pain as part of a comprehensive pain treatment program. They are taught valuable coping techniques including relaxation training, cognitive restructuring, and ways to prevent the kind of catastrophizing and rumination that can make chronic pain worse.

Cognitive behavioral psychotherapy (CBT): a short-term form of psychotherapy focusing on teaching skills and strategies for managing stress and defusing dysfunctional thought patterns that might trigger emotional problems such as depression or anxiety. There are many different types of CBT that can be applied to a wide variety of *settings and populations including dialectic behavior therapy, rational living therapy, rational emotive behavior therapy, cognitive therapy,* and *rational behavior therapy.*

Cognitive restructuring (CR): Therapeutic process used to identify and change irrational or maladaptive thought patterns. A key component for cognitive behavioral psychotherapy and rational emotive behavior therapy. Studies have confirmed the effectiveness of CR in the treatment of problems such as addiction and depression.

Collective trauma: Traumatic distress that can strike entire populations after a wide-scale event such as 9/11 or Hurricane Katrina.

Complex posttraumatic stress disorder (C-PTSD): A more complex form of PTSD that arises due to prolonged exposure to traumatic stimuli or situations. Often seen in victims of long-term physical or sexual abuse, refugees, or people dealing with long-standing conflict or violence.

Complicated grief: Prolonged grief with symptoms much more severe and long-lasting than normal grief. These symptoms often include an inability to focus on anything other than the death of a loved one, emotional numbness, a sense that life has lost its purpose, and a sense of personal blame (such as believing that they could have prevented the death somehow). Often identical to major depressive disorder.

Cyberbullying: Bullying or harassment relying on electronic means such as social media. Just like emotional bullying, cyberbullying often involves undermining a victim's social reputation by spreading rumors as well as posting graphic images taken without the victim's consent. Along with harassment, victims can also be stalked by anonymous abusers as a prelude to physical or sexual violence later.

Cyclothymia: A milder form of bipolar disorder in which emotional cycling doesn't quite reach the highs and lows associated with full bipolar disorder but which can still have a serious impact on a person's life.

Depression: One of the most common mood disorders, depression can be identified by symptoms such as sadness, fatigue, concentration problems, suicidal thoughts and behaviors, sleep and appetite problems, and inability to experience pleasure. Though often confused with sadness or grief, episodes of depression can last for weeks and often require intensive treatment involving medication and/or supportive counseling. There are numerous subtypes of depression depending on the nature of the depressive symptoms that occur. Since many medical conditions can mimic depression, it should only be diagnosed by a qualified professional.

Diabetes (type 2): A medical condition resulting from the body's failure to produce enough insulin. Can produce develop depression-like symptoms such as weight loss, fatigue, and increased irritability, which may be misdiagnosed as depression.

Dysthymic disorder: Less severe than major depressive disorder, dysthymic disorder can still be serious, with symptoms lasting for years before finally being recognized. These depressive symptoms can also cycle with periods of hypomanic moods (a condition referred to as cyclothymic disorder) or else lead to more severe depressive episodes (also known as double depression).

Electroconvulsive therapy (ECT): A controversial treatment of depression and other mental disorders that works by the running of small electric currents through the brain. While it is still unclear why this treatment works, ECT is frequently effective in treating people with severe depression who don't respond to other forms of treatment. Rarely used today due to the notoriety resulting from its misuse during the 1940s and 1950s.

Emo culture: A music genre that is usually identified by the emotional expression, hardcore (and often confessional) lyrics, and the distinctive fashion styles preferred by fans. Similar to goth styles in many ways, emo fans have a preference for studded belts, black wristbands, flat hair, and long bangs that often cover the face. In the same way that goth fans are called "goths," emo fans tend to be referred to as "emo kids" or, simply, "emos." Both goth and emo fans have been linked to increased risk of depression and suicide.

Emotional bullying: Also known as relational bullying. This type of bullying involves undermining a victim's social reputation, often by spreading rumors about sexual or deviant behavior.

Functional analysis: Functional analysis involves having the client and the therapist work together to explore the client's own thoughts and beliefs and how they can shape the way they behave. Clients are encouraged to talk openly and honestly about their depression and explore the way that their mood issues have impacted their lives.

Generalized anxiety disorder (GAD): Prone to episodes of extreme worry, often without any apparent cause. The persistent anxiety seen in GAD can often be so severe that it becomes almost impossible to hold down a normal life. They are also much more easily startled, have trouble sleeping, and have various physical symptoms including headaches, sweating, and hot flashes.

Geriatric depression: Occurring in adults over the age of sixty-five, for example, symptoms can often be triggered by a growing sense of loneliness and be confused with other medical problems such as dementia.

Goth culture: Inspired by the "gothic rock" of bands such as The Doors as well as gothic horror movies, art, and literature, "goths" could usually be identified by their conspicuously gloomy attitude, black hair, black eyeliner, dark fingernail polish, and other styles intended to imitate the "cultured decadence" found in classic horror novels as written by Anne Rice and other authors. Often confused with emo culture.

Heritability estimate: A statistical estimate of the extent to which the variability of a specific trait can be accounted for by genetic influences. Commonly used in studies of the genetics of depression.

Hypothyroidism: A medical condition occurring when the thyroid gland isn't producing enough thyroid hormones. This can lead to significant health problems as well as symptoms such as fatigue, poor concentration, and a depressed mood. Commonly misdiagnosed as depression.

Internet-based cognitive behavioral psychotherapy (iCBT): A completely online form of therapy that research suggests is as effective as traditional in-person treatment programs in treating depression. Still, much of this research is in the very early stage, and many more studies need to be done to determine whether this kind of online help can become more widely used.

Interpersonal psychotherapy (IPT): Partly based on attachment theory, IPT focuses on relieving symptoms by improving the way people interact with family, friends, and peers. One of the central concepts of IPT is that psychological issues such as depression and anxiety occur due to problems in everyday relationships.

Learned helplessness: A popular theory of depression first proposed by Martin Seligman. Learned helplessness is behavior that occurs when the subject endures repeatedly painful or otherwise aversive stimuli that it is unable to escape from or avoid.

Major depressive disorder: The most common diagnosis for people suffering from depression. Usually identified through episodes of depression that last for two weeks or longer and, depending on how much this depression is disrupting normal life, can be classified as severe, moderate, or mild.

Melancholia (also known as melancholy): An early name for depression often seen in classic literature. Symptoms typically correspond to modern diagnoses of depressive disorders.

Melatonin: Specialized hormone produced by the pineal gland, which cues the body to prepare for sleep. Can play an important role in seasonal affective disorder.

Mindfulness: The process of focusing attention on the present moment through the use of meditation and mental visualization exercises. Originally a part of Buddhist teachings, mindfulness training exercises are now widely used in the treatment of a range of mental health issues such as depression, stress, and social anxiety. Specific forms of therapy based on mindfulness training include dialectical behavior therapy, mode deactivation therapy, and mindfulness relaxation.

Mindfulness therapy: Involving the use of meditation, guided imagery, or mental visualization exercises, mindfulness therapy focuses on teaching people to identify those specific thoughts, physical sensations, and desires that might be undermining their mental or physical health. This means that participants can learn how to take in and accept all incoming thoughts and feelings without resorting to automatic thoughts and beliefs that might be destructive.

Monamine oxidase inhibitors (MAOIs): A class of antidepressant medications that act on the brain by inhibiting the monoamine oxidase enzyme that breaks down serotonin, norepinephrine, and dopamine to make them inactive. Popular MAOIs include isocarboxazid, phenelzine, selegiline, and tranylcypromine. These drugs are also known to cause many of the same side effects seen in tricyclic antidepressants and can also lead to serotonin syndrome, depending on drug interactions. Not commonly used today due to the availability of safer alternatives.

Mood disorders: A broad category of psychiatric conditions that include different forms of depression as well as bipolar disorder. Characterized by disturbances in mood and formerly known as affective disorders.

Omega-3 fatty acids: An active ingredient in certain types of food such as fish, nuts, and seeds, omega-3 fatty acids have become popular as a natural treatment for depression in recent years. Though the exact mechanism linking omega-3 fatty acids to reduced depression hasn't been identified, researchers have found a link between its use and reduced plasma norepinephrine and cortisol.

Panic disorder: Being prone to severe panic attacks, often without warning. Panic attack symptoms can include shortness of breath, shaking, tremors, and a sense that something terrible is about to happen.

Pena: A culture-based syndrome found in parts of Ecuador that resembles depression. Symptoms include crying episodes, poor concentration, sleep and appetite problems, stomach and heart pains, and poor hygiene in severe cases.

Phototherapy: Also known as light therapy, phototherapy involves the use of a bright light to simulate natural outdoor light during the first hour of waking up each day. For people suffering from fall-onset SAD, regular use of light therapy can relieve symptoms after just a few days in many cases.

Physical dependence: A medical condition caused by the adaptation of the body to chronic use of a tolerance-forming drug. With this type of dependence, abrupt or gradual drug withdrawal causes unpleasant side effects that can be life threatening in some cases. See psychological dependence.

Physical bullying: The most commonly known form of bullying involving the use of force or stealing possessions or vandalism to intimidate victims. Physical bullying usually escalates over time, and often involves groups of abusers singling out individuals they consider to be vulnerable.

Postpartum depression: A form of depression often experienced by women who have recently given birth (and which can also affect new fathers). Affecting an estimated 10 to 15 percent of new mothers, postpartum depression can last for months in many cases and can often subside only to occur again in a new pregnancy. In extreme forms, postpartum depression can also include psychotic symptoms, leading sufferers to pose a danger to themselves and others around them.

Posttraumatic stress disorder (PTSD): A condition trigged by exposure to a traumatic stimulus or situation with imminent threat of death or harm. Symptoms can include chronic hypervigilance, flashbacks, nightmares, emotional distress, and depression.

Psychic pain hypothesis: A hypothesis suggesting that the emotional distress seen in depression is equivalent to how physical pain affects the body. Psychic pain leading to depression can act as a warning that certain activities may be harmful.

Psychoeducational training programs: Programs that focus on educating depressed patients about their emotional issues and the barriers they may face in learning to move on with their lives. Training modules can include anger management, relaxation training, good nutrition and exercise, and meditation.

Psychological dependence: A form of dependence that can lead to emotional and motivational withdrawal symptoms due to the reduced ability to cope without the drug or stimulus in question. Most commonly seen in substance abuse, can also account for compulsive gambling and other behavioral analogs to addiction. See physical dependence.

Rauwolfia: A herbaceous bush found in many parts of Asia and Africa. Teas made from parts of the plant have long been used in herbal remedies for depression and mental distress. One of the first antipsychotic medications, reserpine, was developed from the Rauwolfia plant.

Reactive depression: A form of depression triggered by events in a person's life but with symptoms much more severe than might otherwise be expected. Also known as exogenous depression.

SAMe Also known as adenosylmethionine, SAMe is a molecule that forms naturally in the body and that plays a role in the synthesis of key proteins, hormones, and neurotransmitters. This includes norepinephrine, dopamine, and serotonin. Available by prescription in many parts of Europe for decades as an extremely popular treatment for depression, SAMe is mainly sold as a dietary supplement in North America. This has been changing in recent years, however, and it has become increasingly popular as a natural remedy for depression.

Seasonal affective disorder (SAD): A form of depression that is linked to seasonal changes. People typically develop SAD during autumn or winter though mood often improves in springtime. Research suggests that SAD may be due to the reduced sunlight that occurs during winter months.

Secondary traumatic stress: A form of vicarious trauma that can affect family members or friends of trauma victims due to secondhand exposure to traumatic experiences. Can also affect health care professionals dealing with trauma victims.

Selective serotonin reuptake inhibitors: Often referred to as SSRIs, these are the most commonly prescribed antidepressant medications used today. By selectively acting on serotonin receptor sites, SSRIs can significantly boost serotonin levels in the brain while only weakly affecting dopamine and norepinephrine receptors. As a result, they can relieve the symptoms of severe depression with far fewer side effects than other kinds of medication.

Serotonin model of depression: A model of depression based on research findings that reduced serotonin levels in key brain regions can result in clinical symptoms of depression. Has been used in the development of antidepressant drugs that work by reinforcing serotonin activity in the brain.

Serotonin syndrome: A medical condition caused by extremely high serotonin levels in the brain. Symptoms include rapid heart rate, agitation, lack of coordination, excessive sweating, and other more serious problems. Can result from medication interactions as well as inappropriate dosage of medication.

Skill development programs: Programs using an interactive training approach to help group members share their own insights and ideas. Group sessions typically focus on training members to handle anger effectively, forming stronger social networks, coping strategies, relaxation training, and recognizing the triggers that can lead to negative thinking.

St. John's Wort (*Hypericum perforatum*): Extracted from the flower of the St. John's Wort plant native to different parts of Europe and Asia, hypericum has been used for centuries by medical doctors and apothecaries for the treatment of mild to moderate depression. One of the active components of hypericum, hypericin, appears to reduce serotonin receptor density and may also dampen the production of cortisol by acting on the body's hormonal system. At present, there is no clear evidence that hypericum is as effective as prescription antidepressant medications.

Stress sensitization hypothesis: This hypothesis proposes that individuals exposed to childhood adversity tend to be much more vulnerable to later problems, including depression and generalized anxiety.

Susto: A culture-based syndrome found in Latin America that resembles depression. Symptoms include insomnia, lethargy, diarrhea, lack of motivation, and nervousness.

Transcranial electrical stimulation (tES): A more modern variation on electroconvulsive therapy, it involves the running of minimal electric currents through scalp electrodes applied to different points along the skull. Depending on the polarity of the current, electrical stimulation can either increase or decrease cortical activity in the regions where the current is applied. Along with relieving depressive symptoms, tES has also been used to boost cognitive functioning, including improved memory, concentration, and problem-solving ability.

Transcranial magnetic stimulation (TMS): A new alternative to the use of direct electric currents, TMS uses shifting magnetic fields to induce an electric flow in target regions of the brain. Most forms of TMS involve the use of a magnetic field generator, or "coil," that can be applied to the head of the patient receiving treatment using a specialized headband. Along with its value in treating depression, TMS has also been used in treating neuropathic pain and boosting cognitive functioning in dementia cases as well as in diagnosing different types of neurological damage.

Treatment plan: As the name suggests, a treatment plan outlines the treatment goals that need to be met and the type of treatment to achieve those goals. Typically developed in the first few treatment sessions by the therapist and client working together. Treatment plans are continually revised during the course of treatment to address successes and setbacks as they occur.

Tricyclic antidepressants (TCAs): Including such drugs as imipramine, amitriptyline, desipramine, and nortriptyline, TCAs work by directly acting on neurotransmitters such as serotonin and norepinephrine to increase their levels in the brain. Less commonly used today due to adverse side effects such as dry mouth, constipation, excessive sweating, tremors, and weight changes. More rarely, it can also lead to seizures, disorientation (especially in older adults), and changes in heart rate.

Verbal bullying: A form of bullying involving the use of name calling, teasing or mocking, or other verbal abuse aimed at undermining self-confidence or isolating intended victims from their support networks.

Directory of Resources

HELPLINES

For anyone suffering from depression or contemplating suicide, the following helplines are excellent places to get support.

National Suicide Prevention Lifeline: 1 (800) 273-8255
National Suicide Prevention Lifeline online chat: https://suicide
    preventionlifeline.org/chat/
The Samaritans: 1 (877) 870-4673
Boys Town National Hotline: 1 (800) 448-3000
Trevor Project Lifeline (for LGBT youth): 1 (866) 488-7386
Crisis Text Line: text HOME to 741741
ImAlive Online Chat: https://www.imalive.org/

WEBSITES

While most cities have local resources that can be found through your family doctor or mental health organizations, here is a list of online resources that can be accessed for more information.

Anxiety and Depression Association of America (ADAA)
www.ada.org

An international nonprofit organization founded in 1979 for the prevention, treatment, and cure of anxiety, depressive, obsessive-compulsive, and trauma-related disorders through education, practice, and research. ADAA's website provides online support for millions of people with depression each year and also promotes scientific research and clinical care programs for people in need. ADAA also provides a referral service for local treatment resources and related organizations.

Freedom from Fear
www.freedomfromfear.org

Founded in 1984 as a nonprofit mental health advocacy organization, Freedom from Fear provides mental health advocacy, educational resources, research funding, and community support for people who need help for depression and related conditions. Along with free mental health screening, Freedom from Fear's website lists numerous resources including internship programs, treatment centers, and online information on a wide range of topics relating to depression and suicide.

Medical News Today
https://www.medicalnewstoday.com/

One of the world's best sources of information on medical issues and available treatments, Medical News Today also has a comprehensive website on a wide range of mental health issues, as well as information sheets on depressive symptoms, diagnosis, and treatment options. The site also includes a knowledge center outlining the latest research into depression and suicide.

National Alliance on Mental Illness (NAMI)
www.nami.org

Founded in 1979, NAMI is the largest grassroots organization of its kind in the United States. Providing education programs in thousands of communities across the country, NAMI also has a toll-free helpline allowing people in need to access information and support on local resources.

National Institute of Mental Health (NIMH)
https://www.nimh.nih.gov/health/topics/depression/index.shtml

A federal scientific research institute funded by the National Institutes of Health and the U.S. Department of Health and Human Services,

NIMH is one of the leading federal agencies for research into mental disorders, including depression. Along with summaries of the latest research studies, NIMH's website also provides basic information on depression, including statistics, and numerous recent publications on diagnosis and treatment as well as links to many other organizations providing services worldwide.

U.S. Department of Veterans' Affairs (VA)
https://www.mentalhealth.va.gov/res-vatreatmentprograms.asp

The VA offers a number of different treatment options for eligible veterans seeking help for depression issues. Both outpatient and residential (live-in) programs are available at VA sites across the United States where veterans can receive inpatient and outpatient therapy, family counseling, medication for psychiatric conditions, and first-time screening. Special programs are also available for women, veterans of recent deployments, and homeless veterans.

Books

These are books that might be of help in dealing with depression and some of the underlying issues that can be contributing to what is happening.

Treatment Guides

Cobain, Bev. (2007). *When Nothing Matters Anymore: A Survival Guide for Depressed Teens*. Free Spirit Publishing.

A hard-hitting guide for depressed teens and their families. Provides facts and clears away many of the misconceptions surrounding teen depression and suicide. Written by a psychiatric nurse who is also a cousin of Kurt Cobain who ended his own battle with depression tragically.

Greenberger, Dennis, Padesky, Christine, & Beck, Aaron. (2015). *Mind Over Mood: Change How You Feel By Changing the Way You Think*. Guilford Press.

Latest edition of a seminal classic by some of the leading authorities in cognitive behavioral therapy. Provides a common-sense program for overcoming depression, social anxiety, and low self-esteem.

Knauss, William J., & Ellis, Albert. (2012). *The Cognitive Behavioral Workbook for Depression: A Step-by-Step Program*. New Harbinger Publications.

A treatment guide from one of the pioneers of cognitive behavioral therapy. Offers a range of exercises and advice on disrupting negative thinking and developing a more positive mind-set.

Solomon, Andrew. (2011). *The Noonday Demon: An Atlas of Depression*. Scribner.

This book explores many of the different perspectives about depression from medicine, literature, art, and history. A fascinating look at the many forms of depression and how it affects people around the world.

Strosahl, Kirk D., & Robinson, Patricia J. (2017). *The Mindfulness and Acceptance Workbook for Depression: Using Acceptance and Commitment Therapy to Move through Depression and Create a Life Worth Living*. New Harbinger Publications.

Written by the therapists who cofounded acceptance and commitment therapy (ACT), this is a revised edition of one of the best classic treatment guides available for people with depression.

Williams, Mark. (2012). *The Mindful Way through Depression: Freeing Yourself from Chronic Unhappiness*. Guilford Press.

This book explores the use of mindfulness training to help people with depression learn to cope with their symptoms and move on with their lives.

Personal Stories

Some of the best advice that someone with depression can get often comes from people who have endured depression themselves. Here are some excellent examples.

Fard, Nima. (2010). *One Survivor's Guide to Beating Depression and Thriving Thereafter*.

This book describes one survivor's journey through depression as well as provides common-sense advice for people looking for help.

Thompson, Tracy. (1996). *The Beast: A Journey through Depression*. Plume.

A frank and eloquent autobiography by a journalist whose harrowing experience with depression from adolescence well into adulthood is covered in a way that only an investigative reporter can truly describe.

Index

About the Author

Romeo Vitelli received his doctorate in psychology from York University in Toronto, Ontario, in 1987. He spent fifteen years as a staff psychologist in Millbrook Correctional Centre, a maximum-security prison run by the Ontario government. In 2003, he went into full-time private practice, and he remains an active blogger and author. His previously published books include *Self-Injury: Your Questions Answered* and *Substance Abuse: Your Questions Answered,* both a part of Greenwood's Q&A Health Guides series.